Taha

The voice is our way to freedom of the soul.

Thank you for coming to Emotional Loadn

Shelly

My Horses,
My Healers

by

Shelley R. Rosenberg

Written with Beck Andros

Foreword by Linda Kohanov

Bloomington, IN

authorHOUSE®

Milton Keynes, UK

AuthorHouse™
1663 Liberty Drive, Suite 200
Bloomington, IN 47403
www.authorhouse.com
Phone: 1-800-839-8640

AuthorHouse™ UK Ltd.
500 Avebury Boulevard
Central Milton Keynes, MK9 2BE
www.authorhouse.co.uk
Phone: 08001974150

First published by AuthorHouse 10/4/2006

ISBN: 1-4259-6639-X (sc)
ISBN: 1-4259-6638-1 (dj)

Library of Congress Control Number: 2006908422

Printed in the United States of America
Bloomington, Indiana

This book is printed on acid-free paper.

Cover art gifted to me by Nancy Coyne.

I dedicate this book to the gift of experience.
If we are willing to share our stories with others,
then we can heal and help one another.

Acknowledgements

Sandy Hogan, you made this come true by introducing me to the writer I collaborated with, *Beck Andros*. *Vesna Mitrovich*, through therapy, you gave me the gift of my own voice. *Dr. Dehra Glueck* and *Laurie Christensen*, you never gave up on me. My Epona apprentice group, *Lori, Sarah, Lisa, David, Mufasa, Anna, Ruth, Missy, Kathy P., Cathy H., Kathy S., Dulce, Deb,* and *Karen*—through you, my peers, I can relive the night Telly literally touched all of our hearts. The *Epona staff* and *Eve Lee*, who told me about telling truth without stretching it. *Jessica Paul*, you received my whole first draft as a gift. *Belle Shook*, you pushed when I was not willing to move. *Rebecca Paradies* and *Kathleen Barry Ingram*, you saw the truth when I was doing my best to hide it.

My dear friends, *Linda Kohanov* and *Steve Roach*. *Linda*, when others said it would never happen, you never gave up on me. We talked, we shared, you trusted me to finish. *Steve*, you have treated me like a sister and part of a family like I had never experienced.

My tall four-legged family—*Laramie,* her son *Telluride (Telly)*, and *Avatar*. My short four-leggeds—*Boboli Boxer, Mini Cooper Bloodhound*, and *Harrison Professional Bloodhound*. Many tears wet all your hides, and many hours of pure love linger among us.

Thank you, all of you, for listening, reading, crying, and laughing.

Namaste.

Contents

Foreword

It's like finding water in the desert. You're meandering through fields of shriveled cactus, taking each step on faith, reciting oasis prayers in a land intent on challenging your very survival, when you catch the first whiff of something green. Is it an illusion, the trick of a mind melting in the trances of an unbridled sun? Or is it something real and true and lifesaving?

When I first met Shelley Rosenberg in the mid–1990s, I might as well have been following a mirage. Or maybe, more accurately, searching for a mythical being: A horse trainer who knew much more than me and was still honest about what she didn't know, someone willing to ride into the unknown and explore what others considered impossible. At first she seemed like all the others, someone qualified to drill me in the well-established, yet certainly dynamic, tenets of classical dressage. Over time, however, something unspoken changed my mind. Something in the way she took on the challenge of my troubled stallion, his mare, and their premature foal gave me the confidence to ask this woman, whose art I could never touch, to collaborate with me on new ways of relating to horses. Shelley not only proved she was up for the task she actually became essential to the ongoing evolution of my training program at the Epona Center.

Now that I think back on it, she did have much in common with Melanippe, the mythical mare-headed goddess of ancient Greece. Shelley always maintained an air of mystery about her, mostly because like any horse in human form, she preferred the silent language of gesture and intent. An extended conversation with her was, like an Arizona thunderstorm in May, an unpredictable event, though certainly as invigorating. She was, quite simply, more at home with her equine friends, though she didn't put up with bull from either species. And like the magnificent dressage horses she rode in on, she seemed to look right through you, to the core, with a piercing gaze you might take as judgmental until you got to know her better and realized she didn't waste a lot of time mulling over the mundane affairs and personality quirks of humans. She was with you when she was with you, and when the lesson was over, she was giving her next student the same unwavering concentration and support.

In fact, Shelley's intolerance for human drama (which others found intimidating), was refreshing to me. At the same time, she wasn't one to shrink from a true crisis of conscience or a sincere emotional challenge. Here was a woman, I thought, who had truly lived through something significant, something that was still changing her life behind the scenes. Here was a woman who knew how to find, no, *create* an oasis in the desert. She was willing to dig deep, put some effort into drawing those life giving waters up to the surface—and sharing this hard-won, soul-quenching elixir with others.

The book you're holding in your hands is the fruit of that labor, a tempestuous journey she took with the help of her horses. Shelley's willingness to chronicle her own search for fulfillment (in a world that seemed to plot against it), her candid portrayal of injustices she witnessed and endured, her honesty in exploring her own moments of weakness and self-doubt at times adds up to the impression that you're digging a deep and tenuous well with her—the feeling of dirt mixed with sweat and a few cactus needles stinging your arms isn't always pleasant.

Shelley insists that the horses who carried her along the way saved her life more often than she might have saved theirs. But I know that in reality, they saved each other. Through their mutual efforts to regain freedom and dignity, Shelley and the horses she worked with over the years have set a precedent for the equestrian world to take a long hard look at longstanding abuses of both species.

There is tremendous courage and compassion in this book, enhanced by the thoughtful, graceful collaboration of writing partner

Beck Andros. I, for one, am both humbled and inspired by Shelley's story, and her willingness to tell it. As she ceaselessly, unflinchingly shines that electric gaze of hers inward, seeing through to her own fluid core, she ultimately challenges us to do the same. It's hard work, plain and simple, but the rewards are forever overflowing.

—Linda Kohanov
2006, Epona Center at Apache Springs Ranch, Arizona

1
Horse Intervention

At midnight in the Tucson desert where my home is, I can step into the indigo dark by feel, needing no light to help me find my way across the drive and down the well-worn dirt path to Telly's paddock. In the soft coolness of this late hour, I always leave the house to come out and check a final time that the horses and barn are secure and quiet, to be sure they all have water. A coyote sings in the foothills of the mountains in the distance. The scent of sage drying in the desert, the particular soft sound Telly's hooves make as they move through dust to meet me—these are gifts.

Telluride, whom I named after the Colorado town, is very tall and dark, and a hint of moisture reflects back the moonlight that reaches into his brown eyes. Running my hand over the pinto landscape of his side, black and white, I know I am a woman kept by horses. They provide me a place in their particular sanctuary and presence to let go for awhile, of what might be broken in me. They offer me a way to heal with them. They are sure and constant and always ready to hear a story I need to tell.

Taking one breath after another with my horses—and you must breathe with them if you want to understand their rhythms and emotions—I can settle myself, become calm, take stock of my surroundings. We can't lie to each other, my horses and I. We know the price of such deceits, and the time it takes to regain a balance. They are incapable of pretending to be brave or of avoiding being scared. When they are curious, they examine the thing that they fancy is new, and when happy, they run and buck for joy. They are aware that I am human, not one of them. My reactions to my own surroundings can be strange to them or seem far braver than they might be able to muster. They take me into their herd because I stay with them and want a place in their circle, and I offer them freely what my humanness can give: protection from predators, kindness, and a place with me. They ask of me only the simplest things—food, water, brushing, and consistent behavior that they can count on. I ask more of each horse than is fair, time and again. Companionship, a listening ear, a soft neck to bury my face in, a competitor worthy of my profession as a horse trainer, a friend. They stand ready, puzzled by this human woman, but willing to be with her. They are strong medicine for me.

Horses are extremely curious, and not always to their benefit. But by putting themselves forward into situations that are new or different, they are by nature interventionists. I began to salvage myself from sexual abuse in my childhood and early adult life through their particular ability to intervene. Horses, and especially the stories they bring to me as their trainer, are an antidote to the pain and isolation sexual abuse causes. They do not leave or ask me to be anything but what I truly am, one emotion or interaction at a time. As a child, I learned how to fear everyone, to trust nothing. Horses staunched the flow of those toxins and showed me, by their pure and frank reactions to my emotions, how to go forward. I could rely on their own consistency and over time be myself with them. They react to authentic behavior from your heart. They don't know what to do with anything else.

My story about my life with horses, sometimes simple or intensely subtle, tell about the healing medicine horses have brought me—it is so concentrated and strong. But what I want to offer you is not just a collection of horse stories, a methodology for training horses, an ultimate set of secrets to horse-human relationships, or a telling about my own sexual abuse and trying to recover from it. I want to show you how horses respond to their world, and how I have taken some life instruction from it.

As a survivor of sexual abuse, I found myself without a definition as a human. I was without purpose, without meaning, and just going through the motions of my life. I hurt and wanted nothing more than to hide away. Sometimes I still do, but because of my horses, so much less often. I learned to ride early as an escape and a means of finding comfort and safety with animals that accepted me as I was—raw with emotion, confused by appearances, and shy of my own kind. This is how horses are with their own kind. Their emotions ripple right under their skin, they are curious about a shape or thing or experience they are not familiar with, and a new entrant to their herd will always be given time and scrutiny before they are accepted. And it's all okay. They do this purely and without worry that there is any other way to be.

I have spent my life with horses, eventually becoming a horse trainer and riding instructor. Horses were my true teachers, so I tell my story through them. They are why I stand and speak. They are my touchstones and bridge to my own kind. They help me heal myself and go into human relationships a little stronger.

Each horse has brought a different story and new people to me, deepening my understanding of life, of connection, of the courage to reclaim myself. In my work with each horse, I encounter issues from past training, and issues with the humans who bring them to me, which can be very complex. Humans and horses can interact well or very badly. The horses challenge me to be fully present with them and listen. I work to understand their definitions and requirements. I have learned to respect their boundaries and to behave truthfully around them. They won't respond to anything less. Should I expect anything less in my own human life, they might say, I will miss the point of being myself and learning how to live with others.

Of course, it's not as easy with their people, my clients. I found I needed to learn a new language to be human with humans, or rather to adapt my own language to be more clear and careful. But my horses are teaching me about this, too.

I tell the story of my day to my horses through my body and voice, actions and intentions. Their gift, their medicine if you will, is how they listen to the story. Subtle or strong in their reactions, I learn through their bodies what is an honorable response in me, and what they find false. Slowly I can build a balance.

Their own stories flow through their movements and their interactions, with their riders and trainers, and with me. One horse at a time, and finally one person at a time, they teach me to be fair and how to trust when trust is earned.

It is taking the risk to tell our stories to each other that can heal us.

Many of us, women especially, write of our relationships with horses as life-changing. Horses have become wizards of higher truth for us, it seems, perfect companions for young girls and middle-aged women seeking something deeper and stronger than the day-to-dayness of life, work, and growing old. Others, brushing wizardry aside, make much of some sort of sexual tension or reason inherent in women talking of and riding horses. In that, my story is similar. There is certainly a sexual component—although the horses play a specific role, not the one reserved for them as somehow surrogate sexual objects for blooming young girls who ride bareback on a hot summer's day.

It's just not that simple.

For one thing, an animal that is a thousand pounds of muscle ignites more fear than passion in most of us. You learn to respect, and set aside, your fear of horses in riding, or you will never give them a leader to follow. Horses don't respond well to weakness; it threatens their own survival, so they will not give up their strength just to follow you to something that could be life-threatening.

Compare a little girl sitting in her grandfather's lap to the same small child riding atop a horse—which would you choose as an image of safety? To almost every child, the comfort of a grandparent's arms of course, the embrace and softness and acceptance, providing the deepest sense of protection and care. Stories read at bedtime. Love and trust. Unbreakables.

The horse, by contrast, conjures flight and panic—a burst of crazed energy that can explode in one intake of just the wrong scent of bear or lion.

Telly and I know how wrong both images can be, the one of horse as only a bundle of wild instinct, and that of child as a being utterly trusting of the warmth of a grandparent's arms. Stories about these images aren't that simple.

Standing with Telly in the dark, he will always nuzzle my arm. He may be seeking a carrot, but perhaps he reaches for the safety that the scent of this human he knows he can trust offers him. Our story together is complex and our sureness of the strength we can offer each other surrounds us in the night with comfort.

My love for horses, and their intervention in my life, started many years before I could own one of my own, perhaps even before I needed their uncanny ability to intervene for me.

In late 1967, growing up outside of Lansing, Michigan, my best friend Joanne Clarke seemed far luckier than anyone I knew, to have an entire family who rode, each with his or her own horse. Joanne's family boarded their horses at Bob Carn's stables. Bob was a well-schooled horseman, or so he seemed to me, someone to look up to. He was a very big man with huge hands, kind, not the sort of person to make a small girl feel threatened despite his stature. Joanne had a horse that didn't interest her any longer as she'd grown as a rider past the horse's talents. The Quarter Horse mare was named Bubbling Echo, a bay with two white socks and a long blaze down her face. At fifteen hands (a "hand" in horse measurement equaling four inches), she was a giant to me. I was in love with everything about her. She smelled good, felt better, and snorted when I came to the barn. The best greeting is a horse snort.

Being near her stopped the sensation of time passing. From the top of her back the world was all mine. Where Joanne was a good rider, I was only a passenger, a lumpy human without balance holding on for dear life. I've since named those days when I knew nothing at all about riding the "kick and pull days," because I only knew how to kick Echo to go, and pull on the reins to stop.

I worked hard babysitting to save enough money to buy Echo from the Clarkes. The Clarkes generously offered to pay her board for me, or there would have been no way I could have afforded her total care.

When I handed over my money for her, she was already pregnant from Mr. Carn's sixteen-year-old buckskin Quarter Horse stallion. So Echo was not only big, she was extremely *round*. Sometimes I would take a lot of time to groom her until she gleamed—others I would just grab her out of the pasture, scramble up on her back, and gallop down the dirt road from the barn to the 7-Eleven. I would buy a Slurpy, inhale it, and then ride just as hard back to the barn, thrilled to be going so fast. She would run and run and run with me, as far as I wanted to go. I had no real tack to speak of, no saddle or bridle, just a lead rope tied to Echo's halter to make reins. We were both wild and glad of it.

The way other people can have remarkable eyesight or a heightened ability to hear the smallest sounds, I have a keen sense of smell. It has been that way since my earliest memories. Echo smelled of the earth on her hooves, the rich mustiness of her hide, and the sweet grass on her breath. To this day, those are the scents of comfort and freedom to me.

I had a few friends at the barn, two of them being the Carn's kids. Rick was a year older than me, and his sister Lori a year younger. Rick was only slightly more interesting to me than Echo. Alright, not true. I was a girl, and like every other girl near my age who came into the barn, I had a crush on him. I was absolutely sure he liked me as well. Every day, we would ride down the road to the enormous sod farms that grew emerald turf for the suburban homes of the Midwest. Once there, we would slide off our horses and walk and walk, trailing their lead ropes behind us, sometimes holding hands. If there was anyone there who might see us, we would just walk along, only talking with our horses and each other. We were enjoying the beginning awareness of each other. Normal kids, normal crushes.

My other life, outside of the barn, was different and not so carefree.

My parents, my brother Ron, and I lived in Lansing. Visits to our grandparents' house in Detroit were easy to arrange and regular.

And Ron and I dreaded them. The abuse started when I was two years old. I was very small when my grandfather began his forays into my room.

Somewhere in the time I spent with Echo, I learned a particular kind of reprieve could be had from my grandfather by breaking something in me, like my arm. The first time I broke something and learned this, we were supposed to be leaving for my grandparents' house and I was in a panic. I dreaded the thought of a visit with the man who created such horror in me. I had no wish to sit in my grandfather's lap. After so many years of his touch, I knew what his lap contained, and it wasn't safe.

When I knew I was about to visit that place, I would go out to the barn several times the day before to stockpile the smell and being of Echo in myself, as others might lay in water or provisions for a coming storm.

Echo's belly had swelled to an extraordinary egg-shaped, hard-to-ride width with her coming foal. On this particular afternoon, sun sparkled off water droplets in the air from the irrigation systems that shot moisture over the sod fields. Rick offered to trade horses with me so I could ride a little faster for a change instead of waddling along at Echo's pace.

Chester, his chestnut Quarter Horse (the Carns were good at naming their horses solid and obvious names), moved easily and freely, swinging along faster, now into jog then lope. Before I knew it, we were flying through the back pasture at a full gallop. I don't remember slipping off Chester and flying through the air, but Chester's muscles rhythmically sloughed me off his back and I sailed. I fell hard on my arm and the ensuing snap told me without doubt I had broken the bone. Rick, seeing me fall, urged Echo to go faster so he could reach me and help.

Facing skyward, sun beating into my open eyes, pain throbbing in time with my pulse through my arm, I felt everything in my life stop to hear just one thought—I didn't have to go to that place.

I would learn to seek pain to give me this safety.

My parents no doubt saw visits to my grandparents as a way to regain some of their own time, to visit the friends they had in Detroit, or as an anticipated respite in which they could leave us with my grandmother and grandfather, and give up the responsibility of kids for awhile to be just a married couple in their own house without us. Did they know what happened under my grandfather's watch? I may never know. The question itself, without an answer, makes me feel even more trapped. If they knew, and could help but didn't, would that make them monsters? Could they have been as frightened of him as we were? I don't know. I suspect they were being parents as best they knew how, but something so sad starts in me when I try to imagine adults who would not intervene for children if they did know this was happening.

My grandfather, Alex, probably hated children. At the very least, he considered Ron and me his private playthings.

The house was stunningly ordinary. No one would know from the street what went on inside. An intense anger simmered under that roof, coming to its own particular boiling point ever so slowly and cunningly, in the night that filled our room with blackness.

My grandmother, Ida, had a huge garden. Released from the car, we'd race there to play until dinner. Anything to keep out of my grandfather's way.

Ida would make dinner, and sometimes we would eat outside in the garden. The sound of crickets, fireflies appearing low near the grass as late afternoon sun turned to dusk. My grandfather would loom at the table, eating, waiting. After dinner, the ritual was a shower or bath for the kids and then an early bedtime for all of us.

On the worst nights, my grandfather would insist on giving me my bath instead of Ida. I would go, dreading his smell and the weight of his breath on me.

The landscape of fear is regular and regimented: a flight of stairs, fifteen steps in all. Three steps, turn to the right, twelve more. At the top, the bathroom, two bedrooms. Seven steps to the right to our bedroom, or twelve more beyond that to my grandparents' room where their twin beds kept their own secrets. I knew this count of stairs and steps by heart, so often did I get the chance to wait as he approached.

Bath time. This is how it happened, time and again. I would begin to act up and scream when the water started filling the tub. He would swirl a hand in to check the temperature. It was humiliating to wash in front of this man, worse to have him touch me, explore me. Screaming until my whole body melted into the sound, I wanted to vanish or drown.

Ida would rush up the stairs, thinking he was just not good at this chore, arguing with him as she entered the bathroom. *Let me take care of it,* she would say, *don't get the child upset, Alex; you don't have to do that.* Arguing. Screaming. He would storm past her and down the stairs, disgusted at me and her, and no doubt frustrated, because I knew by the strength of my body's revulsion, and his continuing insistence to cause it, that he liked this chore, a lot. For a moment, as she picked up soap and rag, the ringing in my ears would fade away to a buzz, and my body would begin to sense the simple reality of warm water again. My grandmother would calm me as I have often calmed a terrified horse. One breath at a time, one soft word after another. The different touch that brings no fear, just comfort.

Fifteen steps up. Three, turn right, twelve, turn right. Seven footfalls to our room. Sometimes Ron and I hated each other as kids. Sometimes we still do as adults.

He was older than me by three years and eleven months, which felt like ages older then, and I think the hate we held for each other germinated in those secrets we each had to keep to survive. I wanted Ron to save me. Ron wanted me to tell what was going on. I think it might have been happening to Ron. But standing over and guarding the secret was my grandfather—in his presence, there was no possibility of safety or telling.

My grandfather let us both know that if we told anyone any of what went on, we would die. Simply that. We would die. He didn't say he would personally kill us or hurt us in any way. Just that we would die.

We never doubted him. Some truths are told to you in only a few words. They have weight and consequence. I knew I would die. So Ron and I created a silent, unified front of mutual hatred for Alex, and in the process, for each other. Knowing the only way we would survive at all was to stick together, we at least made sure we slept in the same room. Witnesses for each other.

As I said, bedtime in that house came early, sometimes as early as seven in the evening, and we would usually try to fall right to sleep or at least fake sleep. But as the small hours after midnight approached, we could both feel his footfalls on the wood stairs. Three, turn, twelve, turn, then the last seven. The door whispered open. Ron would pretend he was sleeping. But he knew it was no dream that my grandfather was opening my mouth with his huge hands, pushing my lips inward, keeping a thumb on my lower lip, folding it over my bottom teeth so they wouldn't rake him as he positioned his penis in my mouth. I struggled and moaned, but what could Ron do? A conspiracy of silence in this wretched room.

Here in the present, I know Telly and the other horses in my care for training are as secure as I can make them for the night. I settle on the couch to rest, too tired to go to my bedroom and formally get ready to sleep. Here, my eyes close and I drift into half-dream, dark, then light, brighter, now blinding sun, burning in front of my eyes, too hot to see clearly, the crackling dry of desert growing louder, throbbing.

My mind draws a shape for me on the back of my eyes; a horse in a round pen who darkens into what I know must be mustang, wild, and far too alert. I begin to fall deeper into dream and now can hear it, too, what frightens the horse. The beat and whir of some large machine approaching through the air. The horse turns his head to me, signals with twitching ears and bunched muscle the panic we both feel. He paws, drops his haunches and spins. It is a helicopter and it dips lower and lower over the pen, rotors slicing this furnace air, shadowing the brightness. I can't stand upright or breathe or reach the horse. The mustang races the circle of the pen without stopping until sweat pours from his flanks, like clear blood flowing.

I crouch frozen in sound and fear and time passing, maybe days or only seconds. Then a new image forms. Hay in piles and stacks on the ground, a bounty for the horse to rest and eat, as if my mind is trying to conjure up sustenance and comfort to this wild creature. Still the horse runs. I can only watch and feel his exhaustion in my own shoulders and back. It takes great strength for me to remain still. The image changes again, and now the mustang grows thinner with each circle he makes, hip bones sawing sharply through his skin with each stride, as he weakens in spirit, draining heart and energy, almost spent. I think that the liquid in the soil under him is not sweat at all, but his will made water, lost and ebbed away into the dirt. I inhale and hold my breath and he stops, finally, heaving. We both taste how tired he is. How spent I am. We are past caring, just breathing together. Leaving our wrecked bodies, we float free, he to vapor; me, as I open my eyes, to my room's surroundings.

Horses come to me in all conditions—thin, scared or scarred, old, not ridden and out of shape, worried, talented and confident, young. Riders come in other shapes and conditions, and owners of horses in still more. I try to care for the students and the owners, but in my deepest truth, I know that the horses are my first concern. I feel I must protect them, to intervene when they need me. Sometimes when I am teaching a student, I can feel myself come close to the horse's skin, where I can feel his fear or confusion. My stories are about what I have learned from taking what I feel in the horse and trying to rejoin it to the human, to understand the nature of the abuse or bad training or relationship that isn't working and change it.

When I discovered that first time at nine years old how to break my arm and avoid the visit to my grandfather, I glimpsed safety. This safety hurt of course, but nothing like the alternative. I would break my wrist again five months later, falling off Echo onto the driveway, intentionally placing my hand at the proper angle for damage. In a strange way, I have always felt I owed Rick something for giving me the gift of this hard safety technique, which was my first learned method for escape.

When I was twelve, my grandparents moved to a new home in Florida. They wanted the sunshine, they said, and Florida was no doubt an improvement over Detroit winters. I had accidentally broken my knee just before that Christmas vacation when we were to go visit them in their new home for the first time. Now I had to go because I wasn't old enough to stay at home in Lansing by myself, and my parents and Ron were going, and it wasn't a consideration to hire a babysitter to watch me. I was going with them, like it or not. The escape I instinctively used when I had to be with my grandfather was to leave my body so I couldn't feel or smell or think about what was going on. I see horses do this, too, when they cannot stand to be spurred on any longer, or do not understand the commands and increasing intensity of their riders' anger or frustration. Their spirit leaves, and only their body remains moving.

Now as an adult, I can and do leave my body in this way, and have learned to use it as a technique in training horses. If I can diminish my awareness of own physical self, and lessen the separation between me and the horse in my mind, I can almost enter the horse's body and feel out the answer to what is confusing him in my cues. But practicing this kind of separation has cost me, as it has a way of creating emotional scar tissue between me and others. I can depart myself and become something else, but how do I get back to trusting others of my own kind again?

For the past thirty years, I have let myself go to that suspended other place when the humans in my life crossed my scarred landscape and frightened me. But with the horses I teach, unless I need to leave myself specifically to feel the insides of their bodies and muscle memory, I stay present and learn. They have stories, too, many of which I'll tell here. Through them, through what they have suffered in owners' or other trainers' hands, and even through the tangible absence of knowledge I can never have about their experiences before they reach me, I am learning that we cannot change the past and don't own the future. I don't know what will happen to them when they leave me, or what causes the humans in my life interact with me the way they do, good or bad. But my horses and I can move and change in our present. We can start a new story that is right here and honorable.

Sometimes in a lesson with a student who does not understand a concept I am trying to get across, I might stop and tell them a story about myself or about what another rider has done, or about a horse that I have trained in the past. This is part distraction from the confusion but also part of the instruction. Sometimes it is just a sharing of our words that can break us through to a new place where we can heal a single scar that prevents us from relating to each other.

Horses have been my way to freedom from pain, out of fear, even to the truth. I want their stories to begin a healing for anyone who is ready to let in an alternative way of experiencing the world.

I sold Echo when I learned how to ride well enough to know I needed a more talented horse. I was ready to move on to competition. I knew enough to tell Echo from my heart that her horse work needed to continue with another girl, someone like me whom she could show how to run and be wild with joy. I sold her to a family with four young children who looked eager to love her in just this way. If only we could intervene more often for the humans in our lives in this way, and find the environment that will suit them so they can thrive.

Any horse knows that of all the night predators, the worst are fear and loneliness. You cannot drink, eat, or rest if you are afraid. You need a herd to help you watch out the long night, to help you survive. Here in this present darkness outside my barn, my horses stand closer together with me and breathe out their stories to strengthen us. We can offer each other a view into healing if we risk sharing our lives' truths with each other. As we pass the time in company like this, we can rest in the comfort of our horse and human herd. Intervention of the kind that can save us is as close as the warmth we share, skin to skin.

2
Mustang Running

What we do to young horses affects them forever. How we handle their ears or their faces, stroke their bellies or the insides of their legs, whether we tighten their girths too roughly or yank on their heads with lead ropes, what happens to them when we trailer them, how we introduce them to strange objects.

In a nutshell, being handled by a human frightens them. If the handling is instructive, they can overcome their fear to the benefit of their later behavior—if they trust us, that is, and we've been honorable in the lessons. If not something small but very essential, way deep in the foundation of who they are, starts to fracture. One incident that causes a behavior is intricately interconnected to another, and before we know it, we've helped to establish an entirely new learned behavior in the horse. Call this a pattern—of trust or mistrust, of sureness that the thing that hurt them once will always hurt them, or that in a particular person's presence, they are always safe.

My grandfather's handling of me laid down a mesh of scar tissue that I would try to break through and re-heal, unconsciously, over many years of interactions. Between twelve and sixteen years old, I struggled through school and relationships with kids my own age, with my parents, and with my brother, with whom I longed to be close. Nothing seemed to work. Don't hold me, don't touch me, but all the time, I wished for them to please understand me and save me. By the time I was sixteen, I was ready to tear away from home and school and pursue the only things that had ever given me peace—horses and riding. I was taking with me a learned need to flee that broken trust, and creating a pattern of reopening my own wounds. My horse life was where I could leave reality and be a child, free to give and receive love, as Echo and I did. But it wasn't enough. It takes great patience, work, and heart, to restructure the foundation of a being—horse or human. And in the meanwhile, if we don't know how to create other, better patterns, we will lay down incident by experience by interaction a silken web of entrapping behaviors.

I was sixteen. On the inside, thanks to my grandfather, I was more adult than child, and yet more child than child. On the outside, I was frightened, worried, and busting out of my skin with desire to move away from Michigan. I wasn't ever the best student, and had begun to dampen the hurt and difficulty of fitting in by getting high at breaks between classes out in the woods near the school—talking my way through or just scraping by in my classes.

But intervention of another sort happened, and I was offered a way out. I'd begun to study dressage riding in earnest and to learn jumping. My trainer, Lenora, was moving her entire string of horses, from Michigan to her new place in Washington State. I had talent, Lenora knew, and she and her husband Garrett offered me and my horses, Reflection and Innovation, a place on the portion of a fifty-acre cattle farm they were leasing in North Bend, Washington. The ten-acre section had been turned into a commercial horse facility sometime in the past, and offered a good barn, indoor and outdoor arenas, a very small house, and pastures. It sounded so ideal. I would be a working student—along with my shy friend Jill, three years older and training in the same barn in Michigan.

My mother set the terms of the deal. I needed to get my economics teacher to sign a letter stating I'd completed his class, the last *required* class of my high school education. She knew what this meant—I'd need to be present each day and study hard because this class was difficult. I could leave early from East Lansing High School and my parents would let me move. I don't think my parents, now long divorced, will ever realize the reprieve they granted me.

It was as if, having run out of options in a dead-end town, I'd been offered the last spot in a wagon to the frontier. If only I met this last requirement for passage, I could be free.

Up until then, I'd given school exactly enough effort to barely pass my classes and get back out to my horses. The economics class would be hard for me to get through, and the instructor had a reputation for his tests. The pressure of passing tests and graduating then, as now, are excruciating for me. Even a horse show with a dressage test—any class—can cause me to panic and shut down if I don't manage the pressure and self-doubt. I know now, but didn't then at sixteen, that many people who have had some type of sexual abuse or other trauma in their lives can suffer far more of this affect under stress.

I decided, because my direction was clear, that for the first time in three and a half years of high school I would really study. Ron was the brain of our pair, the pride of our parents, the diligent one who is now a psychiatrist in Detroit, and a published author. I chafed at being in a classroom.

At sixteen, I had no way to share or talk about what I'd been through, no way to bond with kids my own age. How could I tell these things to a girlfriend? And when? In the school bathroom over a cigarette as we applied blue eye shadow and snapped our gum? To a boyfriend? When would I do that? Over a Coke after school, or gingerly before he kissed me a first time? Wait, I have something to tell you, Roy or Jim or Mason or Lee. How would I possibly start? What saving or healing power could anyone have for me when I didn't trust a soul? I didn't even know why I didn't trust my peers except that I wasn't *like* them any longer. An outcast. Oh, I tried to fit in—normal sports team things like softball, or winter sports like skiing, group things that kids can do to make friends. But I wasn't "Shelley" enough anymore to make a place for myself. Kids can tell when you're different, even if they don't know why. I was a herd of one, and I was very lost.

Remember how sides got picked for a dodgeball game, and the last person the team picked? Was it ever you? You're lucky if it wasn't; you would be one of the popular ones. I wasn't. I sometimes see myself still standing on a gym floor alone, sunk in that particular form of isolation. I don't understand why we let this sort of survival of the fittest team-picking occur. Kindness, or at least fairness, would be picking the teams before games, and then reading off the lists in an orderly way, each weak person having a chance, each strong one having to endure and support the weak. I wonder what the value is in reinforcing the social hierarchy that culls the least popular from the herd. Horses seem to do it—without lists, they exclude a member with a simple clarity. Near the newly cleaned water trough, for example, the water sparkling and fresh, the lead black mare flicks an ear at the gray mare in lower herd standing who noticed the trough's condition first and wants to drink. The lead mare only adds the swish of her tail, and plainly, the extra silent gesture communicates to the lower mare, "Get lost." Perhaps humans and horses share this drive, or innate need, to cull out the weak.

But now, fitting in didn't have to matter anymore. I knew getting a passing grade meant my release. I hedged my bets, and took the class pass/fail so I could "pass" with as little as a D. And for whatever reason, knowing how much my passing in school meant to my father, who still cared that his daughter go off to college, I knew taking the class pass/fail *also* meant that only the passing, not the letter grade, would be recorded on my transcripts. My chances for college, to him, would be intact.

One spring afternoon, near the end of the class term, my mother flatly reminded me as I came into the kitchen from school, already pulling on my boots to head out to the barn, that we had a deal. I needed to provide her with a letter from my teacher that I'd passed, or I wasn't going. The end.

As if I could forget.

The weeks passed, the day of the test came, and finally, I'd done all I could.

The afternoon I approached my economics teacher for the letter, I sidled cautiously to him as a prisoner might a jailer. I tried to read the canny look in his eye. He came around the desk, sat on the front of it, and nonchalantly handed me my grade. I hadn't passed.

The grade, only a D–, wasn't good enough to get out early. And responding to his look, I gave back one of my own—a look I now recognize from the work I've done with wild mustangs adopted for rescue, relocated and in rehab for human adoption—the look of white panic, of being trapped in a fenced and wired paddock, all horizon and landscape shrinking until it is lost. I couldn't stay here; my heart, beating wildly, begged release.

Then he reached slowly into his desk drawer and removed the cap from the fountain pen he was so fond of using to make the elegant slashes on papers. I watched his hand and it seemed that I saw him change something already written there. I was confused. Next, he took a sheet of school letterhead, wrote a short note for my mother, folded it in half, and handed it to me. He didn't speak. I only looked away from his face briefly to scan the words; unsure I'd read that I'd passed, I read it again.

I don't believe he ever knew what he did for me. I don't always know from a horse or a rider when they're struggling with me if either one understands my intent is truly only to help, despite the corrections. But I can understand, and feel, the release that comes with acceptance.

I felt it then for the first time. When I breathed in deeply, the air felt as it if held more oxygen. I was free.

I can only imagine what my high school graduation might have been like. A warm, green, and humid Midwest afternoon, caps and gowns shiny black in the sun, parents proudly fanning their programs and waiting for the roll call of their son's or daughter's name. I can feel it. That liquid on their skin isn't perspiration from the heat, but liquid potential, beading on their arms and under those caps, crackling energy in the open air over the congregation of folding chairs, soon-to-be graduates waiting to be unleashed on the summer, on the rest of their lives.

My destiny was something else entirely. In my mind's eye, I can pause over an empty chair where I might have sat. But if I peer closer, I can see it's not empty. It's full with the absoluteness of my absence, and a relief so pure and tangible to me even now that the memory almost has a taste, it is so sweet.

I went to Washington to become one of the world's best riders and trainers, for I knew only horses could give me true joy, and I surely couldn't afford to imagine failure. To my parents' way of thinking, I was Shelley, the black sheep, bolting for the high country of the Northwest to "become a horseback rider." My brother went to medical school.

I can imagine what my Jewish father might have sounded like talking to his circle of buddies.

"So, Ron is going to be a doctor," my father would say.

"And what about your daughter, Sid?" one of his buddies inquires next, speaking with that certainty that all the children of these men who are friends should do well, *will* do well.

"Oh, Shelley…" My father drops his head a little, "She's going to Washington."

"*Wash*ington?" a friend says, "Kind of far away, isn't it? Not much rings a bell there, Sid." Nervous smiles appear on the faces of the group.

Understand if you can that to these Michigan men, Washington must be a backwater place. It's west of the Mississippi, and well— it's just plain west of anything, for god's sake.

One buddy rescues another, knowing how alarmed Sid must feel by all this.

"Which college, Sid? Whitman? WSU? She's good with horses. She going to be a vet or something?"

Sid pauses, tries to give the truth his best spin.

"I think she's trying to find herself."

"She's lost?" one friend chuckles, liking the joke, "I thought you said she's in Washington."

The banter of good friends; they're all just trying to help out one of their own.

Sid looks away, then back. It's not easy for him to talk about, even less easy to understand.

"She's riding horses," he says. "She's going to be a trainer."

The circle gets very quiet.

Finally, one of the braver ones offers a release for all of them. Just a word.

"Oh."

The conversation might go on long after Sid can stand it amiably, but not long enough for the truth to form. That will take time and the years passing. Only I know that, and only now, at a distance. It wasn't as pretty or easy as just "learning to be a horse trainer."

Patterns. I would start to create the worst of them. One relationship at a time.

I was sixteen. I was free.

North Bend, Washington was a landscape of miraculously green forests, benign weather after Michigan's snows. Nothing but horses for me to bury my life in.

I was fresh out of school, and would need a car in Washington. But my parents insisted that I was too young to drive across the country alone. Lenora and I arranged that when she came back to Michigan to pick up the last of her horses and my own two—I had a bay dressage gelding named Innovation and a bay jumper mare called Reflection—we would drive the distance in each other's company.

Her husband Garrett was a machinist, a welder, and was already in North Bend working. The tiny house and other outbuildings were built by a previous owner, not the cattle owners, and it seemed a perfect place to run a thriving training business. Lenora now trained horses for clients in the Puget Sound area, from Everett to Seattle to Olympia. She gave lessons to many of these clients after they got off work, and on weekends when they drove up to North Bend.

My job, along with my friend Jill's, should have been general barn maintenance and exercising of the clients' horses. Jill had just completed a course of study at an accredited riding school in West Virginia called Meredith Manor, which had a long tradition of training riders and future riding teachers. She was as eager as I was to work with Lenora in a training barn. Our reward, or pay if you will, would be to get coached as young trainers through a lesson with Lenora each day, and to be schooled on the better horses in the barn.

Lenora, a petite doll of a woman, carelessly banded her long dark hair into a pony tail each day. She was icy and seldom approachable, different from my Michigan experience with her. We quickly learned that there would be no training epiphany. We weren't clients any longer. We were now the hired help, or worse.

So began what felt like servitude. In three years time, we would take only three real lessons with her.

Lenora owned three Great Danes. When we arrived from our long trip, pulling into the driveway with the truck and trailer, Garrett let the dogs out of the house so that they bounded forward to the car. They engulfed the smallness of Lenora in gray muscular hides and elegant long legs. I envied her, owning these beautiful dogs who threw themselves in her path to greet her. It was a Sunday afternoon, early summer, and Garrett stepped through the screen door and came out on the porch of the small house holding a drink.

I took my stuff out of the truck to the porch. He ushered me in, smiling, holding the door open as I lugged my bags through and inside.

"Put your things in the room next to Jill's," he said.

The bedrooms were just down a two-foot hallway, and directly opposite Garrett's and Lenora's own bedroom. The house was no more than a worker's cottage—three square bedrooms, kitchen, and a sitting room in a tight, single story. My room was clean and empty: on the bare wood floor, one twin bed, a chair, a lamp. I settled my bag under the window and tried to open it for air, but I only dislodged old paint flakes. A torn screen leaned against the wall by the window.

Lenora flopped into a kitchen chair.

"Jill's running errands," she said. "She'll show you the routine when she gets back. I'm exhausted."

Jill worked at a local pizza shop, 6 p.m. to 1 a.m., to earn spending money. Lenora didn't pay us in cash, only lessons in trade for work.

"But basically, the schedule's like this," Lenora said. "You and Jill need to get the barn chores done before my first morning clients. Jill's up by 4:30 a.m. You'll help feed the horses and clean the barn. The arenas, indoor and outdoor, need picking, watering, tending every day. You have Sundays off."

Because there was no other barn help, Jill would tell me later that it was better to work for free on Sunday so Monday's chores and stalls wouldn't be twice the work and keep us away from riding.

"At 11:00 a.m.," Lenora said, "You'll get your lesson from me."

This was supposed to be the payoff for the work, a lesson for each of us. We seldom got it, as Lenora was seldom free of clients—but even if she had the time, she'd beg off saying that she needed to go in and sit awhile. She'd watch Donahue or a soap opera.

But we didn't seem to mind then if we missed the lessons. We had the horses to ride in any case, each other for company, and the work—we'd ride almost all day, and again after the night feeding if we could. Jill and I were horse crazy together.

Lenora kept teaching hours all day, and in the evenings as well, when her clients came out from Seattle. She didn't ride anymore. She had broken a leg in a fall and told everyone it made riding unpleasant, even though she could still ride. Mostly, she stood and talked to the riders, coaching from a distance.

She had one very special student, a young girl with a Grand Prix horse. That student would be arriving any moment for a lesson with Lenora, now that she had returned from the trip to Michigan.

Lenora pushed her chair back. "I need to get back outside."

And that was that. I was here.

Garrett made me a sandwich, and I ate I listened to Lenora's instructions to the rider crossing the air from the indoor arena.

By nightfall, everything seemed in place and right. I'd come a long way.

Everyone had a work routine, and it seldom varied. After horse chores and riding, Jill's pizza job in the evening kept her out until 2 a.m. Three years older than me, with her own car and a grown-up's sense of how to take care of herself, she was my best friend and I missed her when she was gone.

Garrett worked all day in town. When he came home, he would drive up to the house and roll to a casual stop. Sometimes as he closed the door and brought in groceries or whatever else, he'd call to me to join him for an iced tea on the porch. Sometimes finding me there already, finished with some chore or other, he'd put his work things down and settle next to me to talk.

It seemed to start slow for me, a kind of hunger for someone to care about me, love me. Almost as if I'd been starved for so long I didn't recognize what the absence was. I'd never had a man's attention in any straightforward way, so I enjoyed Garrett talking with me or seeking me out after he came home. I wanted Lenora's approval, and Jill's company.

By 6:30 p.m. every evening, Lenora came in briefly for the dinner I'd help fix with Garrett. The Great Danes got underfoot, but because they were as big as miniature horses and elegantly clumsy, I couldn't help but love them.

One evening, Lenora motioned to Blue, the female Dane.

"You want her?" she stated, not really asking, "You can have her."

I took the gift as a sign that I was more than help, becoming family maybe. We sat down for dinner, my hand dropping to the dog at my side, feeling the smoothness of her coat. And just as casually, not knowing what it was at first, I felt something brush my leg; Garrett, brushing his leg against mine under the table. All the while Lenora talked about her day and moved the food around on her plate.

My heartbeat skipped and I sucked in a breath. This man who was married to my boss, who helped to pay my bills, seemed to like me. What did it mean? And my next thought trampled the first: This isn't right. Of course I knew it was wrong, he was married; this just couldn't be okay.

But it was heady stuff. When my heart let go and I breathed deeply, I thought his touch meant I was accepted.

Evening after evening, a kind of dance was taking shape. First it was small touches, unseen. Next, glances across the room or the table or the barn aisle.

Slowly I let myself examine this feeling of being wanted, loved perhaps. I felt special, maybe even different from Jill, somehow growing prettier, more feminine. I never let her know, never talked about it in the chilly morning while we mucked stalls and doled out food for the fourteen horses now in training. I only told Blue my secret. She followed me everywhere, and grew heavy from my clandestine offers of table scraps saved for her. She looked pampered and moved slowly in the summer heat. I would press my face to her gray-colored neck and remind her she was mine, all mine.

It was a chilly morning, two months after I had arrived in North Bend with Lenora. I'd finished dragging the arena footing back to level once more, and drove past the barn to park the tractor in its spot out back. As I passed, I saw Jill walk a dripping horse out of the wash stall. I hadn't seen my Dane all morning, but she often followed after the two males to sleep in the cool of the barn. I walked back to find Jill and we both froze hearing the shrill screech of Lenora yelling at Garrett.

"Damn son of a bitch got to her. I told you to keep an eye on her," she said.

Garrett mumbled. Lenora thrashed back into the barn. After a minute or two, she stomped out, dragging a grain sack that looked heavy. Something moved inside.

We ran closer to look, to help if we could.

Lenora's fury boiled up like thunderclouds and the blackness of it engulfed all of us. Her face white with anger, her lips pressed and nose flared as if she smelled something disgusting, she rolled down the edge of the bag to show us the contents.

Thirteen mewling Dane puppies, so fresh their ears stuck flat to their heads and their eyes were shut tight. From the barn, we could hear and see my Dane barking and barking, throwing herself into the barn aisle as far as the short fixed chain Lenora had clipped to her throat would allow.

Without a word, Lenora closed the sack with a twist and cinched it with a piece of bailing twine. She dragged it behind her past a paddock off the barn and to the water trough. Heaving once, deceptively strong for her size, she lifted the mass into the trough, newly filled that morning. Bubbles rose from the water, and she pressed down with all her weight to keep it on the bottom.

It didn't take long.

Jill tried to comfort me between chores; Lenora scowled every time she saw me wiping my face. I tried to comfort my dog. By early afternoon, Jill was ready to leave for work and the dog still wasn't right. I begged Jill to take me to the vet on her way to the pizza shop, and she called ahead to tell her boss she would be late because of a family emergency. Garrett and Lenora were nowhere in sight. We snuck my dog into the back seat of her car, where she laid panting and anxious on an old blanket.

The vet listened to the events we spewed out and intuited from the dog's behavior and the timing that probably she still had a puppy left inside. He whisked the dog into the emergency. Anesthetized, they found and removed a last pup from my Dane, the small tan thing dead all these hours.

"Go home, Shelley. We'll call you—she's too groggy to take home now," the vet told me.

Jill and I left without my dog, and didn't speak all the way to the farm. She hugged me as we parted in the driveway, then got back in the car, turned it around, and headed onto the road again.

When I called the vet's office back, it was dinner time and I got their answering service. It took the vet a while to return my call.

"I'm sorry, Shelley" he said. "She just never woke up."

I had lost not only my first dog ever, but my friend—and her puppies. She had held my secret and paid dearly for it. Who would hold it with me now?

It was a summer weekend afternoon. The strong sunlight had started to mellow for fall but the air was still dry, redolent of heat and fir and cedar.

Garrett set the ladder against the house; he had the paint stirred and ready in the cans. We'd scraped off old paint through the morning hours, and now reached the rewarding part where the color, fresh white, went on and the house reminded you stroke by stroke, board after board, of its structure, its thirst for color.

Lenora worked at the barn with Jill, out of sight in the cool indoor arena. I climbed up the ladder to do the highest boards. Garrett spotted for me, steadying the ladder at the base.

In mid-stroke, I felt the ladder shudder ever so slightly under me, and turned to look down. Garrett climbed one rung at a time, until he stood behind me, one rough hand on my leg, sliding up my thigh to the edge of my shorts. He climbed another rung, and pressed himself along the length of my back, reaching around me to hold my breast. He nestled his lips into the tanned nape of my neck.

I tilted my head, my heart racing. I shouldn't. I knew I shouldn't. But I wanted more, there, be soft, there. I closed my eyes, and with one clear thought as pointed as broken glass, I realized what was happening. I stiffened.

"Stop it," I told him. "This isn't right."

He took his hand away, and with a soft brush of fingertips down my back, then over my calf, he retreated to the ground. He gazed up, smiling. I couldn't breathe.

Later, in my room, I remembered how it felt and a kind of confusion seeped in. I was okay for this night. But did I want safety? I was sixteen. I didn't know I was lost, that the rules were changing. I had no desire to hurt Lenora or lose my job. Remember, I was sixteen and a minor.

But when the next night fell, and the door to my square small room opened to let in Garrett's shadow, then Garrett, I thought I wanted it to happen all over again, to be held, touched, kissed. His bulk filled the room, and soon his body engulfed mine.

I believed I was going to be the one person he truly loved and wanted. At sixteen, this was my first sex with a man who wasn't doing this to hurt me.

Weeks passed, and in the afternoons, or nights again after the afternoons, the secrecy and urgency and frequency increased. Garrett always used a condom. It happened most often when Jill was at work, and Lenora taught her evening lessons in the arena. While he laid on me, he watched for Lenora through a small chink in the outer wall of my bedroom. So watchful, I thought, that surely he'd keep me safe.

You believe the thing you do by routine can't hurt you because you know the pattern. That's how complacency works. Until the day you step into the hornet's nest on the trail you've walked a hundred times without incident.

One early fall morning, Lenora left the farm to begin a trip she'd planned to Michigan to see her parents. Jill and I ran the place through our usual and efficient routine. We enjoyed the solitude without Lenora, and at noon, hopped up on our own horses to school by ourselves. At 4 p.m., right on time, Jill went into the house and got ready for work in town, and I got ready for my routine with Garrett. It wasn't desire or something special anymore. It was sex, and he expected it. I had come to dread it now. I was sixteen, and these were now the rules of this place.

After the sun went down and Jill's car pulled away, Garrett led me to his and Lenora's room, and slowly undressed me. In this room, he tried new, riskier things with me; I didn't fight. At some point, suddenly, I fell dead asleep. I didn't remember drifting away or being tired. I just wasn't in the room any longer; it was as if I was sucked out of my body—a dissociation that happens even today. It felt like an instant, and then I startled back to consciousness. How long I stayed like that, inert, I didn't know. Garrett now snored on his back, one arm flung across his face.

I hadn't heard Jill's car pull up to the house, or the door to the bedroom open. Everything occurred dreamlike and wrong.

In the dark, Jill came to the bed. Garrett had given her instruction, too, it seemed, similar to mine, and unknown to us both, to come here on this particular night.

I realized she must have been coming to this bedroom for a long, long time. Only now we were both here, and both secrets were exposed.

Afterward, we couldn't talk about it. Jill and I worked, rode, tended horses. That other part of us held its silence, avoiding trespass or light. But it lurked there, all the time.

Lenora's two breeding stallions lived in separate paddocks that connected to a single large pasture that only one stallion at a time was allowed to use. They stayed separated because as stallions, Lenora told us, they would fight and could kill each other or damage themselves, leg or ribs crushed in anger, into ruin.

We would never remember how it happened. Did we leave the gate open by accident? Did Jill or I turn just so with the muck cart, leave a gate open just enough as we worked side by side and cleaned their paddocks, that they had enough room to slip past? In an instant they came together. We froze before running for halters and lead ropes to get them apart.

They sniffed, stood erect. One pawed the ground. Nothing more.

With ease and relief, Jill grabbed one, and I took the other. We led them quietly back into their paddocks just as Lenora appeared from the barn.

She had seen what happened. Her scream spooked both stallions so that they wrenched the leads from our hands and kicked out, running away to the end of their separate paddocks.

The sky fell. We were sure we'd be fired, have our horses booted out onto the road. Instead, as payment due for breaking her rules, she looked at us once, then spun away, never saying a word after the scream. She froze us out; simply stopped talking to us. For weeks it continued like this. There was nothing like Lenora's shunning. We were nonpersons, invisible.

For three months we worked like wraiths in the barn, silently piling manure, dragging arenas, cleaning tack, riding horses. Cautious, edgy with Jill and she with me.

Lenora kept her silence continually for that three months—like a vow she took that we just didn't exist. We would have begged her on our knees to talk to us if it would have helped, but that wouldn't have made a difference to her.

Garrett continued to take each of us in turn, somehow more easily now that we were punished goods. We could do nothing but endure Lenora's shunning and wordlessly be taken by him without telling.

A whole year passed, finally, and Lenora forgave our transgressions. Grateful isn't enough to describe what the reprieve felt like to us. New horses arrived, some left. And the start of the second year found us still firmly, secretly, in Garrett's keep.

Lenora's star pupil, the beautiful young rider with the Grand Prix horse, had wealthy parents who had just finished building her a facility in Auburn, Washington—closer to Seattle and Bellevue than Lenora's North Bend location. The pupil would ultimately grow up to own and teach from this facility, but in the meanwhile, her parents invited Lenora to manage and staff the new horse barn. It was state of the art—new arenas, a track, spacious stalls; a trainer's dream place. Lenora left first. Garrett stayed behind for a few extra months to finish moving the horses.

That's when Jill and I started to fight. I refused to be left in North Bend with Garrett, and so did she. But we didn't say why, or exactly what worried us—we just argued over who'd been here longer, or who had less to lose in the move. In the end, I left first because Jill had a job in North Bend to keep. I couldn't wait to leave Garrett behind.

After Lenora moved, all her clients followed to Auburn, too. Garrett transported all the horses in the barn over that three-month period, and the second year became the third. We worked as hard as before in the new location.

In that third year with them, I finally broke. I had had a few months without the routine of daily sex with Garrett to give me enough space in which to pull myself out of a stupor. When he rejoined us in Auburn permanently, the pattern solidified all over again, and he expected Jill and I to continue as we had before. I tried to leave my body as I had learned to do to endure the sex, but I just couldn't any longer.

Jill, wanting to escape both Lenora and Garrett, dated a farrier named Jeff, and left the farm, staying away as often as she could manage. I told them I needed to get my education going again, and enrolled that fall at Kent Community College. I wasn't interested in school; I was just trying to meet someone and start a relationship, so that I could have a person and a reason to help me leave Garrett and Lenora.

I took classes guys would take, like arc welding, so I could meet men; I met and liked a young guy named Joe. I wasn't at the new barn more than six months before I told Garrett and Lenora I had good news and better news—I had a boyfriend, and they could have their house to themselves because I didn't need to live with them any longer. Garrett fumed, but he couldn't do a thing. Lenora acted indifferent, but she smiled at Garrett when I told them.

I stuffed my small belongings into my bags and moved into a place Joe shared with his sister and her husband. That was temporary, just to get out. Eventually, we settled into a tiny apartment of our own.

I only went to the farm to work.

Was it something Lenora did or simply the desire of the beautiful student's parents to take back management of the new facility? Maybe her parents smelled something wrong, some behavior that wasn't right for young women to be around. Imagine what that must be like, to have parents who suspect and intervene.

Lenora and Garrett hadn't been running it long before the owners asked them to leave the new farm. They moved on to work at a Thoroughbred barn. The dominoes tumbled and Jill moved away, too, with her farrier, and married him.

It all happened so fast. Joe asked me to marry him, and I thought about it. I was dying of that thirst, almost past knowing or caring in ways that mattered; I'd drink any water, sweet like attention or rank like flight, to survive.

While I thought about escaping through Joe, Lenora asked me if I would take on a small project showing three trick horses back in Michigan for a client she knew. She couldn't go back there. Maybe I could. The client owned a little horse van, outfitted and painted for taking his two stallions and a mare touring to perform their circus-like talents. I said yes. My life was rewinding itself back to Michigan.

Joe agreed to go with me. As we traveled through Michigan on our way to the client, I impulsively made him stop so I could check in at the barn that belonged to Lenora's former trainer, Mr. Grant. I can't say why; maybe your instinct knows better than you do what you really want. The sweet Michigan day smelled of leaves and pumpkins, brisk puffs of wind lifting my hair. I found Mr. Grant at the barn, and after talking and catching up about Lenora, I asked if he had time while I was there to give me a lesson. I was hungry to be on the back of a good horse with a good trainer teaching me. He said he had the time, and the lesson passed quickly and felt like salve on my being. This is where I belonged, in a facility with a good trainer.

"You know, you ride okay," he told me. Understated praise from a professional. I could hear the coded meaning, one rider to another, that I was very good.

"I have a working student position. Would you be interested?"

I thought about it. Now that I was back in Michigan, where I started, I felt older by more than the years I'd spent away. I was more wary, having learned and endured things that hurt me, and then healed up only enough to go on. Wound, scar, break wound, heal scar. Was I working in a pattern of hurt and avoidance? Or was I now moving forward with an ear cocked to the pain, letting it guide me?

Joe had put out feelers before we left Washington and had gotten a job offer in Lansing to do arc welding. If he took it, and I took this job with Mr. Grant, I'd be commuting from Lansing to Brighton daily. Not good for us as a couple, I thought. But I wanted this horse work more than a relationship. I wanted to train, compete, and win—badly enough that I'd give anything to find the right mix of work and reality and growing up. I would just have to travel back and forth.

"Sure, Mr. Grant," I said. Inside, I was screaming *"You bet your life I'll take it."*

When Joe and I were settled, I called Lenora and Garrett, and asked them to ship my horses back to Michigan.

If I believed that some price must always be paid for mercy, then my release from Lenora and Garrett cost me Innovation. He colicked while traveling, a torsion in his gut, and was detoured to Michigan State University for a surgery that was new then in horse medicine. When I finally got Innovation back, I promised him a year in a pasture to recover. Mr. Grant agreed with me, generously offering me space. But Innovation died the next year anyway, from an adhesion—a piece of gut blocked with scar tissue from the surgery. I was so far into competing by this time that losing him, a horse I loved, was just a break in the wave of my life. I missed him, but I had to focus on the positive, the thing that made it okay to breathe—this work.

So I kept working, and I kept shedding pieces of myself that I didn't need or want to keep. I just couldn't stop moving. I began showing Reflection at third- and fourth-level dressage. My pattern with horses was becoming my only reliable behavior. Work hard, be clear, and recognize the small goals.

I couldn't be as clear about humans or relationships. After a little more time trying to work out a relationship, I called it quits with Joe. I didn't know if I wanted out more than him; neither of us was happy. With Garrett, I had needed to believe that someone could love me. He didn't. I think I had tried a relationship with Joe to see if I could repair what Garrett damaged, as much as to escape. It didn't work. You can't run. My road through these and other relationships would be long, and I'd take a lot of wrong turns before I saw or understood the pattern of them, or my role in them.

So Joe moved far away, to Boston. And since I couldn't afford the rent on what Mr. Grant paid me, I decided to move back in with my father in Okemos, and keep traveling to the barn for my job.

It's been a long time since I was sixteen.

Very recently, after many years, Jill and I reconnected when I traveled to Seattle to do a clinic. On a break between the lessons I taught, we tried to catch up. We've both changed so much. I knew she had divorced the farrier a long time ago, and had found a man she loved a lot. She said she liked my longer hair, that my face is so dark from the Arizona sun; she told me over and over that I rode and taught so well, that she was really glad I still worked with horses.

I brought her up to date about my life and my dressage center in Tucson, about my partner, my work with therapy horses, and about the new mustang we just got in.

"Do you still have horses?" I asked.

"Oh no. No time," she said.

"Do you ride at all? Ever?"

"No," she said, "I'm busy with work and the boys, and I travel with Ray whenever I can. Life is pretty hectic."

At the end of the day, leaving for home, she hugged me and told me she hoped my telling this story would help me heal.

I don't know if she needs to heal or tell the story, as I do. Some things stayed unspoken.

I think of the new mustang my partner and I are working with. This horse gives new meaning to the word *wild*. In the noonday Tucson sun, he'll bolt to the corner of his dry paddock, sides heaving with fright, just because my shadow stroked his flank.

If he could understand my words, I would tell him of my own fear: I was sixteen, I'd say, scarred, scared. Where I sought human comfort and trust, I found a predator. I am a human, and my shadow in this brightness might make you think a predator is near. But I am not a predator. Just a human who cares. You can run; I'll understand. It took a long time for me to heal, mustang, but finally, my own voice spoke out from my terror, and the hands of those who could listen reached in to hold me, without pain. I can breathe now. Touch doesn't always mean hurt.

Sometimes we tell a story, and sometimes a story tells us. You can be so tired of fleeing, that you want to give up caring. Don't worry, mustang. I'll be here. I'll wait until you are ready to hear the simple kindness and truth in my voice.

I'll always tell this story for Jill, for the mustang, and for me. Flee if you must. One of the three of us will always hold the space and the story for the others to return.

3
Transitions

I go to riding clinics to observe, ride with higher-level instructors, and gauge how my training of a horse is going—professional opinion to professional opinion. One week recently I worked with a clinician from Santa Fe, and on that day I was not comfortable in my skin and probably shouldn't have ridden. I had been working my mare Laramie, Telluride's mother, less than usual, duties as the Tucson Dressage Club president and late winter rain making it difficult to use my outdoor arena. We'd come to the clinic because my friend Lee was holding it at her barn, and barn owners try to support one another. Also, the clinician, a German named Gunnar, was rumored to give a hell of a hard workout. Despite my lack of consistent work with Laramie, I'm always game to try a new instructor. Gunnar and I had each seen the other compete; the southwest show circuit is tight and every rider's progress visible and remarked on.

I'd been traveling for the few days right before the clinic, and so my mare had truly languished in her paddock without benefit of the consistent, slow schooling we usually do to move ahead to our next level. Normally, I wouldn't dream of riding her without that preparation; I'd take my first day or two back at the barn to just walk her, feel her muscles, and make sure she agreed that the movement was okay for her. I wanted to avoid resistance in her body. We have a partnership. But I would learn at this clinic that Gunnar didn't consider this a routine one should follow, if one wants to succeed. That was a question for my work and my life: Did I want to succeed?

It's not easy to answer, and sometimes, if you're recovering from something in your past, what success looks like to you can be very unclear.

At the highest levels of dressage, if you want to be here, you have to choose to push on through your horse's reaction to the work itself, which becomes as mentally rigorous as it is physically hard, and to ride through your own frailty and struggling conviction to a place beyond stamina. It is a *choice* because you don't have to go here. At this level, I think what you accomplish comes about through a marriage of your horses's cooperation and your belief in each other, as much or more than from talent. Both rider and horse need to buy into the deal, because it's about trust. Choose any other way, and you risk "just riding" and only scraping the ceiling of the next level.

Not all riders or horses can make the mental shift to the work of the upper levels. My mare might be talented, but without knowing she has something akin to grit and pure determination, I can't ask her to trust me to perform movements that are so difficultly balanced, and tremendously beautiful. I'm not sure I can ask her for something I know could break us both spiritually, if we don't have a mutual agreement that we want to get there. This is my personal wall that I often hit—do I want to achieve these higher levels or not.

The morning's clinic already had casualties. One of the riders who went earlier is a judge I know, and a fine rider. I respect her skill in work and judging. Gunnar made her cry. Eva isn't one to cry when the riding gets really tough, but she now looked slightly ruined in her crisp vest and dark breeches. Her pony tail stuck half out of its holder, and a smudge of dirt streaked her face from forehead to chin where she dragged her gloved hand across the tears.

I walked Laramie into the arena, feeling her stiffness and my own. I had a dozen excuses for why I needed to be slow and soft with my big mare. She expects this from me. Her rules. I need to wait until she tells me she's ready. I believe in this agreement and solidarity between horse and rider.

Gunnar stood slim and razor sharp. "What are you working on?" he asked me as I warmed up, his accent scraping the softness out of this Western afternoon.

"Oh just training level, and it's our first time in a full bridle," I tried to joke with him to ease my own tension. My skill and Laramie's are so far beyond training level it's silly, but I wanted to do anything to get this off on the right foot.

"I don't think so, Miss Rosenberg. I've seen you competing. You don't have any training-level horses."

I had to get serious really quick.

"Intermediare II, flying changes. We're getting three in a row, every stride."

Flying changes are changes of lead, or leading front leg, at the canter. A right lead means the left hind strikes off, followed by the right hind and left front diagonal pair together, and the last leg to touch ground is the right front. Accomplishing one lead change in mid-movement is an achievement for most riding horses, but it is an expectation for all western horses trained for reining, and for any good jumping horse. It's just the beginning of the ladder for the upper-level dressage horse.

"So," he said.

"I haven't ridden her much in the past few days—I'm not sure I should work on changes today."

"Are you riding her? Or is she riding you?"

He watched my warm-up, and then told me to cross the diagonal and begin half-pass. We'd be cantering in a moment. I couldn't tell what was going to happen in this ride, and I didn't like the feeling. I knew through my seat that Laramie wasn't happy.

"She has to be rounder still, more flexed."

I struggled with Laramie to achieve the collection Gunnar wanted from us. I started my canter down the center line asking for the first lead change.

"Oh, now, she's not even straight. Stop! Stop now. Let me get on her."

I halted, got off, and before I could blink Gunnar was up in my saddle and walking Laramie away from me. Laramie visibly argued with him through her jaw and muscles and he tapped her sharply with my whip. I felt it sting both of us.

In a few moments, after several more touches of the whip, he had rearranged Laramie's body. He cantered down the center line with straightness and attention. I could tell Laramie was listening, but she seemed puzzled by the change. No one had asked her if she wanted to do this.

"Your horse is a cow," Gunnar said from the saddle. "She's very difficult. You will not work on changes until you get her straight. She has to listen to you, Shelley. She can do this, but she won't do it without you making it clear that you're in charge."

As I took the reins back from Gunnar so I could remount, Gunnar slipped off Laramie with grace and fluidity. I began to explain my partnership with the mare.

"We work together, Gunnar. I don't like to push her if she's not ready for the next new thing."

"She's ready. It's you who is not. This is where you start *riding*. It's not up to her to determine where you go next, or when. Bring her back tomorrow—we have a lot of work to do."

I left the arena deflated, knowing he'd found the place in my road where I always paused and thought for a very long time about moving ahead. I could tell he knew without explanation that I had stood here often, immobile and then unwilling to make an issue of the work. I am not sure whether I am ready now to be a different rider, or if I will ever be. It isn't a transition I even felt comfortable thinking about. He knew that too. I resented that he'd called Laramie a cow. She's not. And she's my baby. I've done everything on her. To call her a cow is close to calling me lame as an instructor.

Which makes me think about where I got started on this path, and what I ever wanted from it in the first place. When I was nineteen, I joined the barn of Mr. Charles Dudley Grant, and for better or worse that was where I stepped solidly onto this road called "horse trainer."

From nineteen until I turned twenty-three, I worked four of my own horses with Mr. Grant—we called him Chuck—and rode six days a week with total focus. Here I sampled what it would take to become a professional. My path had three basic requirements: Because anyone's potential is short-lived, I would require persistence to succeed. I needed a high tolerance for sameness in my routine, because no matter how varied the horses, I would only make as much progress as the last good ride. And, most of all, I had to be comfortable with loneliness without going a little crazy, because riding one horse after another, patiently and with care, despite its resemblance to a meditation, is still plain hard work with only the horse as your company.

My herd at Chuck's consisted of Billy Joe Freckles, a Grand Prix leopard Appaloosa stallion, whose spots made him look like a Dalmatian; Reflection and Sweet Serenade, my Thoroughbred Grand Prix mares; and Innovation. Innovation only survived my first year with Mr. Grant, before he died of complications from colic surgery. After rubbing myself raw on human relationships in Washington, I now set about polishing myself in this career that chose me.

Chuck was tall and handsome and he liked me. He didn't interfere in my personal life. He didn't ask me too many questions, or worry needlessly that I'd fail. As my instructor, he cared appropriately about me, and checked me when I wandered into some funk that interfered with the work I was there to do. I felt strangely lost in this attention that was just enough, never more or less than what I needed. He seemed to know not to get too close to me, but thinking back, I imagine he must have wanted to reach in and shake me out of myself sometimes. Maybe he respected distance in a person. Maybe he'd been kicked by seemingly trusting animals, and knew better than to assume closeness to a girl-animal like me. No matter; I respected him for letting me engage with him and struggle on a work level, as a horse trainer, and tough out the other parts of my life on my own. His approach suited me. When I was impatient and asked him to show me what success entailed, what it might cost, to let me taste it through shows and the horses, he helped me to ride and train with consistency and to win. He showed me how to teach a horse the circus tricks of bowing and standing with their forelegs on a block; he was energetic and full of surprises. And he rode as well as anyone I'd ever seen.

We traveled and competed everywhere. I'd track behind his rig with my own, hugging his brake lights mile after mile to the next event, still hungry for more. I wanted all the stress of high-level competition, grueling show schedules, and the crazy life around the edges of the wins and losses and movement. Like gypsies, we towed horse trailers full of treasure—our animals and saddles and desire to win and be something more. I wanted to prove something, to train and then finish my own horses into champions, to ride like my life depended on it. Because my life did; it was all I knew, what I felt safest doing, and the only thing I gave a damn about. I wanted to taste the sweetness of getting on the United States Equestrian Team and experiencing the Olympics. My dreams weren't small.

But at some point with Chuck, I stopped believing he was enough of a personality to help me get there. After four years, I thought I'd learned all I could from him, and he wasn't going to satisfy my need to be visible in the horse world. Of course, I know now that no one makes you visible; you either earn visibility or trip over it by some stroke of luck. Someone somewhere notices you, on a particular horse, in a near-perfect dressage test, and you achieve that magical thing called *potential* in their eyes. Then, if you're lucky, they can move you along in your career. They think you might make it, that maybe you can take their expensive horse farther than anyone else has so far. You're worth a risk, and maybe, just maybe, they hire you.

I wanted that return on my investment in this work. As I schooled with Chuck, I thought of other barns I might be at and where those could lead. Chuck gave me advice where he could—when I'd let him that is—but I wanted to run my own place, my way, or push on. I quietly decided I might take on barn management for a small farm in Michigan—Nottingham—to become the resident trainer. But I also applied with an outfit in Southern Pines, North Carolina, whose trainer was part of the Florida show circuit and aggressively pushing for the top. That's what I really wanted, but I'd hedge my bets with Nottingham if I couldn't get on with the Southern Pines circuit right away; Nottingham was a transitional place. I'd train, wait, and keep applying.

On a chilly Michigan morning, several weeks after I'd agreed to go to Nottingham but before I'd told Chuck, I sipped hot coffee and leaned on a fence rail, looking out at the pattern of Billy's spots, only barely visible in the milky gray light. I sensed Chuck come up behind me. He laid his hand on my arm. As if I had an instinct for lightning striking, I shied away from his touch. He looked surprised by my movement, and hurt. I tried to relax back as if my feint hadn't happened, too late to cover for myself. I really cared about him and for an instant wished I could be different. Still, I couldn't keep that feeling in place. I was nowhere near ready to trust anyone in a real way.

Chuck settled in at the rail next to me, leaning into the old wood.

"I know you're going to be leaving sooner rather than later," he said, his words adding curls of vapor to the air.

"Oh," I said, caught out, struggling to find some lie that would sound like truth. "I was going to tell you. Nottingham's just a small barn, but it'll be mine to run."

"I got a call from Jim Ephraim," he said, leaving the subject of Nottingham in the dust. "They're getting the barn ready for the trip south to Florida."

My face flushed red with this outing of my plans, but then why did I really think Chuck wouldn't be familiar with the right people, the ones at the top? He was a well-known, respected trainer. He had accomplished so much with his own work and clients. The horse world, no matter how diverse, is tight and very interested in everything at the top. It watches everyone. And it's very, very small.

"He's not sure he's got a spot for you, but he'll give you a call in a few months. You'll be busy if you get on there. I told him you were good, and you'd work hard if he took you." He snugged his collar up around his throat to keep the cold out.

"You know you don't really have to leave," he said. "We have a lot more to teach each other."

I flashed a look at him, distrusting his words, wondering what on earth he thought I could possibly offer him. He looked away to the distance. I was always on guard for something more in a man's attention, but here it was only his gruff kindness I felt settle over me. How could I tell him I wanted to take what I knew and show someone else, as much to prove to him that he'd taught me well as to satisfy my own desire to be really good? Was I ungrateful? Maybe. What I knew for sure was that this comfort chafed me. It created an almost irresistible burn in my life that made me ache to break something.

"Everybody grows up, Shelley. You're good. Go find that out. If you find that *good* isn't enough, you come back. I can always use good."

"I just need—"

"I know," he said. He turned his head to look out at Billy Joe who had started to walk toward us. The horse's spots grew more distinct the closer he came through the mist, until he stood nuzzling the jacket sleeve of my arm on the fence, seeking a treat. He looked like any other spotted horse, not the great and talented dressage mount that he was.

"Won't get much warmer than this today," Chuck said. Billy lipped for the carrot Chuck pulled from his pocket. Chuck smiled, let him have it, and then reached over to touch my arm again, this time resting a finger there to see if I'd flinch. When I didn't, he seemed satisfied to release me. He put his hand back into his pocket, and walked up the drive to the barn.

I worked double-time over the next three weeks until I could pull everything together to head out to Nottingham. Jim Ephraim hadn't called me directly, just Chuck. So I followed my plan to keep working and wait. Tack trunks full of breeches, summer shirts and dress whites, polished boots, salves and liniments, old ribbons, new horse magazines and clippings from past shows. I couldn't tell if I'd be staying in Michigan or moving south, so I packed as if I needed everything, and all of it was temporary.

The morning came when I hugged Chuck goodbye, both of us standing apart more than we should have, afraid to show each other what we might be feeling. As I drove out, I stuck my arm out my rolled-down truck window and waved. I just couldn't look back.

My time in East Lansing at Nottingham didn't last longer than the snow of that winter. I taught and trained, but the barn offered me little growth, and the owner couldn't teach me enough or give me the latitude to run the place the way I wanted. When I called Jim Ephraim to leave a message to remind him about who I was and that I was still interested in working with him, I didn't expect him to actually answer.

"Yeah," he said.

"Mr. Ephraim, this is Shelley Rosenberg."

"Rosenberg…Oh *Miss* Rosenberg," he said, his tone turning silky. "Of course I remember you. How's Michigan treating you?"

"Okay, I mean, fine."

"Lovely," he said.

"Mr. Ephraim, I left Mr. Grant's barn, and I'm now the resident trainer at a facility—"

"You bored?" he interrupted, "I would be. Why aren't you doing more?"

"That's what I'm calling about," I said. "Do you have any openings for students?"

"What kind of horses are you working?"

I started to tell him about the horses in training at the farm, but he wasn't interested in those.

"I mean *yours*. What do you have? What are you doing with them?"

I told him about my mares. He listened attentively.

"Bring them down. We'll be back in North Carolina in two months. Be here by the end of June."

And so I left. Once more, I couldn't look back.

I started to demand more of myself and my horses. I bought a horse through Jim that came from Waverly, West Virginia, a gelding that gave me a different perspective on what I wanted to do with dressage. My background in horses until then was mostly Thoroughbreds and Quarter Horses, so when I purchased Kingston, my first Warmblood (a horse bred in the bone for dressage work), I made a commitment, financial and emotional, to up the ante on my career. If you don't ride this discipline, or know this particular sport, this type of horse won't be familiar to you. But if I said that buying such a horse with this kind of potential can be like deciding you don't just want to have a car that gets you from place to place; you finally want to *drive*, to taste acceleration and curve and power, you might start to get a sense of it. If you love to really drive, you eventually want to understand what happens with the gears, and practice the right time to shift up or down by feel and sound until it's second nature. You want to meld yourself with something way stronger than you are, and hand-craft each response. A horse bred for dressage, as this one was, can make you feel this way when you ride him. And I cannot forget fashion. At that time, the dressage world had turned its eye from the finer Thoroughbreds to the bigger-boned and larger Warmblood breeds. The look of a small rider perched atop and effortlessly controlling a perfectly mannered, elegant monster of a horse was all the rage.

Kingston was three years old, a 17.1 hand Dutch Warmblood. I arranged the payments with Jim for his $10,000 purchase price, a small ransom with which to begin the gamble on my future.

Jim Ephraim rode hard and drank his meals. But he excelled at his job, and I started to feel myself stretch again as a rider and trainer. We competed in North Carolina, Virginia, and West Virginia shows all summer. I worked Kingston in my free time, getting comfortable with his personality and athleticism. We all knew that when the skies got darker with fall and winter sent the smell of snow and cold as a warning over the paddock gate, we would begin to migrate south to Florida to compete. Then the work day would lengthen to include the warmer nights.

Jim's deal with me included one private lesson each day, and I paid for another so that I could move ahead faster. I knew I was considered a working student, but I tried to give more training in my own work with the horses, and probably absorbed more training from my lessons than most of the students I taught or rode with. I didn't mind the repetition of horse chores and grunt work because I was shedding a skin that had kept me invisible and plain, and radiated something new that other riders and trainers noticed. William Steinkraus, who rode for the United States Equestrian Team for twenty-two years and captained the Team for seventeen years, and rode in five Olympic Games—and his wife who was also a competitive Prix St. Georges rider—came to work at the barn one day and saw me ride. These important dressage riders looked at me, away, and back again. I reached as far out of myself as I could, to circle their orbits and try to close in. I'd enjoyed a good competitive season at the Paddocks in Florida. When we returned to Southern Pines, I attended the breeding trials. I needed to be everywhere and only if I moved and rode and talked to people constantly did I have a chance of making it. For the first time in my competitive life, I not only saw the road ahead—I knew I was on it.

In Southern Pines that summer, Jim had two other working students, and we all passed most of our time in the barn. Between chores, our own horses, and our lodgings, we were seldom anywhere else unless we were showing.

And so it happened on one show weekend that was just like any other. The first day of the show was over, and the sun in the evening sky darkened from a ribbon of pink to a red shawl stretched over the barn. We students bustled through our pre-night routine, which involved cleaning up after the horses and getting tack in shape for the second day's classes. Despite feeling tired, I enjoyed the peacefulness in the barn as we completed chores. The animals chewed hay in their stalls; some were already blanketed, others needed to be. As we mucked bedding, the barn dogs snacked on whatever bits we missed.

Jim had ridden well that day, and now sauntered down the aisle tired and easy and full of himself, suspending his whisky glass of ice and bourbon between thumb and forefinger. I had no doubt he had already refilled it several times. His cheeks were flushed and spider-veined, and his eyes gleamed dark and medicated. He had come back out to the barn to see if we had changed blankets yet, from coolers to heavier rugs for the night. These were fine show horses, and we treated them like the royalty they were.

Jim stopped at Kingston's stall and took a swig from his glass. I was struggling to stash all my gear back into my tack trunk in front of the stall, having just cleaned up my area of the barn, and not liking him standing over me. I wanted to finish and move away from him. I have an instinct for something wild in a person that meant trouble; it had a smell. It wafted around Jim like a rank perfume.

"What all do you keep in there anyway, Shelley?" He stepped toward me, edging into my space.

I stood and placed myself so that the trunk was between us.

He smiled.

I didn't.

He set his whisky glass down on my trunk, then unlatched Kingston's stall door and slid it back. The stall was 12 feet by 16 feet, spacious as stalls go. Kingston could hang out in the back away from all the human intervention if he wanted to. Jim tugged Kingston's blanket off the bar on the stall door as he went through, and moved toward the horse.

"I'll blanket him for you," he said.

Jim's movement into his space caused Kingston to stamp a foot and then fidget. I was the only one who handled him routinely, so Jim was a stranger, and his sudden approach made Kingston anxious. My horse stood taller, ears erect and nostrils wide. I walked quietly into the stall and got in front of Jim, reaching to take the blanket from him.

I talked to Kingston to calm him. "Ooooooo-kay, big man, it's okay..."

Jim pushed past me to the horse's head, readying the blanket as if it were a bullfighter's cape he could fling up and over Kingston's back. Kingston snorted and stepped off to the back of the stall.

"Damn horse," Jim muttered. Kingston stamped again, tense, sensing he had no escape.

"I'll handle him," I said, and put my arm out to stop Jim and take the blanket.

Jim spun on his boot heel, his face so close to mine I could taste the bourbon on his breath.

"*I'll* do it," he said.

There is a certain tone in someone's voice that starts me spiraling into a state of anxiety so pure and sharp that I lose myself. The voice spins me around, knocks me off balance and backward from wherever I am in the moment to a whole other place and time. I fall into space. Light drains from the air. Sound becomes white noise. Then the spinning stops and I realize I am lost. Maybe it is just the very next minute, but in my head time becomes years ago, so real it is present. The voice that started my freefall is now, clearly, another voice that I knew somewhere else. Sometimes I smell something so intensely that this other place solidifies in front of me. Jim's voice was directing me back to someone, someplace known, to a familiar voice telling me just how things were going to be, little girl.

My gut whirled, worry knifing me deep as I tried to break to the surface of this minute to catch my breath. I didn't want Jim to hurt Kingston. I sucked in air and struggled to pull myself back to this place, all the time feeling like I was falling away and away.

In a voice unrecognizable to me, low and furious, I warned him. I had only an instant to get myself in control.

"He's my horse and I'll blanket him."

We faced each other in the stall. He reached out and pushed me away. As if I'd taken one wrong dance step, my foot twisted under me and I fell. When I got back to my feet, I grabbed his arm from the blanket and pulled his hand toward me.

I truly wanted to try and reason with him before my anger took me under, and so I pulled him as hard as I could to get his attention.

"Stop it—I'll blanket my own damn horse. Get out of here before you get hurt. He isn't used to you."

Jim swung his arm back as if he would turn and retreat, but instead brought it in a fist to my face. He hit me in the cheekbone, right under my eye. The pain bloomed white into my forehead and nose. I put my hands up to deflect another blow, but he'd stepped back to the stall doorway and waited there.

"Enough. Get the fuck out of here," he said.

He didn't need to tell me to go, I'd left mentally before I felt his fist; that anger took me far away. I just couldn't leave Kingston and my horses here with him, and I didn't know what I'd do to him if he hit me again. No matter how contrite and sober he might seem in the morning, I'd never be able to trust him.

Morning came and cast a yellow light over the trashed and spent hours of the night. The bruise at my eye and cheekbone had turned a livid purple. I loaded my gear, horses, and any thoughts of making the long list on the Olympic team or anything else into my trailer. Jim could make real trouble for me with a few simple phone calls. And even if he didn't, I would still have to explain what had happened here at the next barn. No show barn manager was going to believe me over Jim. I suddenly realized I wasn't much of anybody yet.

I had enough money to get me and my horses back to Michigan, and that was it. My father and I had had an argument weeks before that left us not speaking, but I called him anyway and told him I had to leave Southern Pines and why. I hoped for understanding, if not support.

"You need to stay there," he said. "Your career won't happen if you quit and leave."

"I'm not quitting. But I can't stay." I knew I had just enough self-esteem to get myself out of that situation with Jim, and maybe enough to get home. I wanted my father to understand, but couldn't figure out how to explain to him that I'd changed somehow and the anger that had been under the surface of my skin would swallow me if I let it out again. Something in my core would explode and burn itself to the surface of my life. I thought about why I'd left Chuck Grant's, and asked myself what had been so damned important that I needed to do. I couldn't come up with a good answer.

I took the horses back home in one long haul, and lined up a job at a tiny farm in Lesley, Michigan along the way. I was turning out to have a true knack for picking the lowlifes in my trade—the owner of this next outfit was an alcoholic, his wife a mouse. I didn't realize it until many years later, in that perfect vision of hindsight, but a certain broken type of human with a resolve to hurt always managed to pull me in as if they were trolling for me. I rolled ever downward emotionally and financially, not knowing where to be or what I was good at. At least the job at the small farm kept me teaching lessons and riding my horses, and gave me a place where I could act as if I was still in one piece. But it was nothing more than an act.

My bank account started to cave in. I was still making payments to Jim on Kingston, but now my current income and expenses left little over to cover them. I fell behind on him. Of his $10,000 purchase price, I had paid off half. So I told myself a story: If I called Jim and asked for time, knowing that under all the bluff and bourbon he was still a horseman, he would spell me for a few months until I could catch back up. I believed he would give me that grace somehow, because he might have thought I'd been good at what I did there, regardless of what had happened. But I was fresh out of grace. Jim's office manager returned my call; Jim wanted me to bring Kingston back.

I remember how loading Kingston into the trailer felt like failure, and every single mile of that drive from Michigan took me farther and farther from myself. I cried like a baby for what I'd lost. Me. Me, young. Me, wanting something huge for myself.

I was a working adult who couldn't even pay for my own horse, the fancy one I was so sure I needed and that was supposed to be my ticket up. How could a professional make it without Kingston, a professional's horse? I was nothing. I knew I would never in my life be able to afford another horse like him.

When I pulled into the stable's driveway, I sat in the trailer until I was sure I could unload him without losing control. I felt humiliated that I couldn't complete my agreement to buy him. In the barn, the other working students were doing their chores, focused as usual. I didn't want to meet up with Jim, or any barn help I knew, and explain what I couldn't understand fully myself. How could I have let such a small thing happen, the interaction with Jim, and let it end what I wanted? Surely it was my fault. I could still remember the panic around him. But now I questioned my actions—did I quit too soon? Did I want any of it bad enough? Why was it so easy to let myself down?

I saw a groom in an aisle way, and without a word, I unloaded Kingston, walked him up to the groom, handed him the lead rope, and told him to let Mr. Ephraim know the horse was back. Then I left. I'd lost myself in this deal. I had wanted Kingston to become something first that I wasn't yet—polished and skilled—and help me get there too. He was the first Warmblood I would have—big, handsome and bred for competition. But as it turned out, I just wasn't worth his time.

I don't think I spoke to anyone for a week after I got back to Michigan, but it could just as easily have been a month. I have no measure for that lost time. I rode my horses, went to bed, rode my horses, went to bed. I had no desire to get better, to be happy, to take time for myself. It was so humiliating to *be* me. I was drowning in depression. I took more and more emotional abuse from the barn's owner. I must have felt like I deserved it, because I didn't argue back. "Look, you can't even pay for your own horses; how can you possibly move on or leave this job," went the script in my head. "Where will you go with three horses?" I told myself that it was important that I keep punishing myself until I realized fully how low and ugly I really was.

When I sold Billy Joe Freckles, my Grand Prix leopard Appaloosa stallion, to Anne Gribbons in New York, I sorely needed the money. I let Billy go for Kingston's asking price of $10,000. That was a lot of cash in the 1980s. I knew I could live on it for awhile—I could get out of this job and just hang on for a few months—even if it felt like I was eating my own young, one horse at a time, to do it.

I took Billie's money and quit the barn, moved my two mares to another smaller barn where nobody knew me, and just rode as a pleasure rider. I got a regular job, as a cashier at a drugstore. Day in and out, customer service, mindless tasks. I wasn't doing what I loved, and I wasn't with my horses. My spirit ached with exhaustion. I carried a stone heart in my chest. At least when I left for Washington from Michigan years before, I knew that no matter what I had to do there, I was going to be with horses, the creatures that made me feel like I could survive anything.

I still can't explain the sustenance they provide me, when I'm able to look out my window and see them. They are peace to me. The simple presence of horses centers me. Without them in my days of ringing up drugstore purchases, I felt weighted to the earth, sinking. I had no idea how to get back to doing horses full time. I wanted it badly enough, this dream of being in my day whole and well with horses and work, but I had no vision or idea of how to get back there, to my life, to peace, to what I knew best. I was pretending to survive, and losing. I needed the animals. I needed to be doing the work I was good at.

It was day two of Gunnar's clinic, and I had brought a new horse, Avatar, because the shoer was coming to trim Laramie's hooves and I couldn't give up the appointment. And I was still smarting from his "cow" comment. I wouldn't let him disrespect me that way again.

Avatar, a big reddish-orange chestnut gelding who was new to my barn, ambled with me into the arena. He was an easy-going guy. We warmed up at the walk while Gunnar finished a conversation with an auditor on the sidelines. I started my trot sitting, riding Avatar's big gates smoothly. My balance was excellent and it felt good to be riding.

"And with this horse, what are you working on?" Gunnar's focus turns to me immediately in full throttle.

"I'm just beginning to work with him. I've had him a few months. I'm not sure what he's capable of yet."

"We'll do changes on the diagonal," Gunnar instructed me. He was obviously not letting up just because I had a different horse under me. If I couldn't do changes with Laramie yesterday, how did he expect me to do it today with Avatar?

"From the walk, take the canter," Gunnar said.

I didn't know if Avatar was balanced enough yet to do it, but I asked, and he lifted and went easily.

"As you come around the corner, ask for his change," Gunnar said.

Just as I passed, Gunnar kicked some dirt in Avatar's path to surprise him into the change. Avatar startled into a huge spook that sent me careening down the long side. My heart landed in my mouth as I gently pulled us back together, and then slowly returned to the spot where we started.

"You could have killed her, Gunnar," my friend Lee said.

"But I didn't. Now ride, Miss Rosenberg. Please."

I was scared and angry. But lead change after lead change, picking up the canter from the walk, things I'd never done with Avatar before happened from my seat, legs, and hands. I knew I wouldn't try this with Laramie. Was it because Avatar was a horse I was grooming for sale, who wasn't mine, and so was okay to risk riding this way? Because I knew I wouldn't be the one who would have to push him through to the harder places and risk failing or disaster? Or was it something else?

"Very nice," Gunnar smiled as I finished a simple change. "You can walk now."

Dreams can seem so real.

In the gentle part of the night, near morning, just before the sun breaks over the mountains behind my house, I often toss in sleep through landscapes of unfulfilled wishes and goals. I pass myself coming and going on a road that crosses over a creek named "might-have-been." I scan the horizon to see where I am in the dream, and then feel my dream dreaming itself and me back to reality. Sometimes my dream frets, even as I look on, as it plays out the drama I've chosen. It longs to stop this show and just be solid and still. *Just listen,* it asks. *If I could live with you in daylight,* it tells me, *and stand with your legs, I would want nothing to do with perfect endings. I am your dream. Take me along. I'm hungry for wild consequences and things that don't work out right. I want to try on hard things like new clothes, one possibility at a time. What changes survives, like you. I want to change. Let me.*

We each want the other's world, and can hear this desire clearly in the transition between day and night, night and day, when we're able to touch the boundary between us, whether ruined or healed by my dream's dreaming and my living. At this place we will always wait, transition, and then move on again.

As a young trainer, my fantasy was to have everything from the high-end, professional horse life—visibility, success, and a place and reputation in which I worked with the only creatures I felt safe with. But that dream shed itself of me the way a horse flicks a fly off its skin. I got back to horses eventually, in a different way. My father rescued me by offering me a chance to move to Arizona to manage a store he owned. It gave me a place to start over and slowly reenter the horse community. My luck would crack again there too, but I'd keep going this time. I've learned that my dreams don't break me in ways I can't handle. They always leave a few good bones intact. I have my barn in Tucson now and a reputation, so I've made it in a way.

If I could do it all again, I might turn to Chuck at that fence in the cold morning and tell him how much he meant to me, and how scared I was about everything ahead. He surely knew something about what would happen when I left. Horse people develop a special sense of coming disaster. Some try to steer our own kind to shelter and help; others lead us to the edge of the cliff and push. Chuck cared enough to show me that I had what I needed to succeed, whether I chose it or not. Jim Ephraim taught me that to speak up and say "no," and still keep going, was a necessary part of my toolkit as a professional.

At Gunnar's clinic I learned that "good enough" might never be enough for some of us. I still don't know if I need more in my own career. But at least at this clinic I learned to ask myself about it without feeling defeated by the question, or feeling as if I'm letting Laramie down. All I can do is try my best, wherever and whenever. Success might just look like a change of lead on an untried horse.

I am grateful for small transitions, in myself, in my horses, in my thoughts. Achieving my dream is a never-ending process, because the very dream keeps changing. We are true partners, my dream and I. We must both grow used to the discomfort of not knowing how far we will go or what we will change into. For a horse, like Laramie, discomfort ends when she is turned back into her pasture and is only a horse once more—not my mount, not my expectation of Grand Prix competition, not mine at all. She is her own being again. And Avatar? I find he never takes my discomfort seriously. He knows at any moment, I might surprise him with a request he's never had before. He'll do his best to do what I ask him. Sometimes he'll succeed, sometimes not, but he'll always get dinner and a rest. To a horse, all such achievements are simple and profound. I'm still learning from them.

4

Human as a Second Language

I tasted my espresso in the darkness. I woke early to the pounding rain on my roof. What little light there is shows the sky roiling with clouds in hues of near black and deep blue. Not much chance to ride today, but like a daily meditation time, my muck fork awaits me for stall cleaning, and the horses expect food. From my window, I watch the heavy downpour soak my dressage arena into 100 by 200 meters of red mud. Later, I'll use my tractor to drag in as much of the water as I can or I won't ride tomorrow either. Fortunately, my two lessons this afternoon are at a barn on the other side of Tucson that has an indoor arena, so no weather delay will stop work there.

One of my students, Sabina, called for a second lesson this week. She is making no connection with her Thoroughbred mare. This means she and the horse can't find a common way to move together. She's given up on her previous trainer, she told me, because she's sure the trainer and the mare, Innis, were on a collision course. After a few sessions the mare was "crowded"—which meant she felt restrained from moving forward or simply ahead with energy. When I watched one of her lessons before I took her on as a client, I could see the trainer driving the horse into a closed set of reins and contact, or closed hands, while simultaneously asking Innis for more movement ahead by urging with her seat and legs. Imagine if you asked someone to approach a closed door at a walk. Now you tell them to break into a jog, and next a run. You are asking them to head straight into that closed block of wood. Your person can't go anywhere because she is blocked by the mass of the door. For a horse, the feeling of being driven ahead with more energy, but without the rider allowing a release to really move, feels like real entrapment. Without "opening the door" so that the horse's energy can truly go forward, from hind end through body through head, the only place the horse can "escape to" is up. She'll rear. Innis had indeed started rearing, one of the more dangerous habits—once it gets established—to correct. Sabina no longer felt confident about the horse and her safety.

I haven't offered to ride the mare yet. I can see the fix and taste the connection and energy Sabina wants to happen so badly, but as a trainer, I can't wave a magic dressage whip and make a rider "get it." Feel, or the sense of what is happening through the horse's body to your own, is not about control, but about your own willingness to risk being vulnerable with the animal long enough to let go of your own stuff and let them move. You need to sense how hard the horse is trying to understand you. Call it one spirit willing to be intimate with another long enough to listen. The horse and human need to find a common language in which to communicate, and it's new to both of them.

I'm in my forties and single, and I've struggled throughout my entire life to be intimate with my own kind. As a trainer, I've had plenty of time to practice the art of listening to the language of "horse," and I'm reasonably good at it. I'm far less good at understanding "human." It's as if "human" is not my native tongue. I take a deep pull on my coffee and reflect. The liquid burns my mouth, a physical reminder in the place where I form words, that I need to be exceptionally clear when I explain the "fix" with my student. I can show her how to connect with Innis, but regardless, I'll have to explain how that works, and words are so hard for me.

I don't know when human became my second language, and horse so much easier. I ran away from home to horses, and I never experienced anything but safety with them, even when they were wild with me. But thinking this morning about Sabina, I remember when I noticed a connection between using the language of horse to reach humans struggling to communicate with each other. It was through the work I did at Sierra Tucson.

I had come to Tucson to run a drugstore for my father, who had several of them. But it wasn't what I wanted for my life. I heard about the opening of a new adolescent care program at Sierra Tucson, a facility devoted to therapy. The adult programs were founded in the 1980s. The adolescent care program and horse facility that would combine kids, horses, and psychotherapy were scheduled to open in the summer of 1991. As soon as I heard about, I felt drawn to the concept in such a strong way it almost overwhelmed me. I went up to the facility before the program opened and applied for a job as an assistant, even offering to be barn help. The receptionist handed me a hefty application, and because I would be working with adolescents, I had to be fingerprinted. It was a serious document and process, and my heart stopped when I saw the space for college education. Remember, I wasn't the best student. College had been my brother's path. I'd taken horses. So to apply for this job, I chose to pretend I had a level of education that I didn't. Somehow, I believed with all my heart that if my experience and skills were right, and if this was my calling, Sierra Tucson would overlook this small lack of a degree and take me anyway. Horses will overlook scars if you can still hold your own with the herd. Maybe my kind would too.

Waiting to hear anything back, I quit the store and took a summer job I had previously applied for at a girls' camp in New Hampshire, where I would teach riding. I knew I had to get out of Tucson's baking heat and distract myself from thinking about this job that seemed made for me. I couldn't just sit and wait there.

New Hampshire turned out to be a good place to pass time. The girls I taught were funny and serious about riding, and we enjoyed each other. But my thoughts drifted morning and night to that perfect job, and in the back of my mind, I wondered what I would do when I got back, if Sierra Tucson didn't want me.

On one of those beautiful blue New Hampshire days, when I was finished with morning lessons for the girls in my riding class, I walked to the camp office for a soda and to check my mail. I ripped open the letter from Sierra Tucson as if it were on fire.

Dear Miss Rosenberg, wrote Barbara Rector, the program director at Sierra Tucson. *I've received your application. I would like to interview you when you return to Tucson. Please contact us at your earliest convenience. I look forward to speaking with you.*

I drank in the words again and again.

Something was starting in my life, and the feeling of anything being possible made my work through the rest of the summer evaporate in surreal, quickstep time. I breathed in the opportunity ahead, exhaled, and summer was over.

In September, as soon as I dropped my bags inside the cool shade behind my Tucson front door, I called Barbara to tell her I was in town, and we set up the interview date. She apologized that we wouldn't start in the facility itself, because the barn for this new program wasn't even completed yet. But the kids' residence and the executive offices stood ready and she'd show me those. We would meet at her office.

I knew I liked her as soon as she extended her hand in welcome. We connected from our first words. Perched on the edge of my chair in her office, I leaned forward and told her why I wanted the job, how I felt I could help kids because of my own experience with incest and abuse, and how horses had saved me. She responded that when she reviewed my background and references, she knew she liked what she read about me and my work with horses, and felt, also, that I was well suited to this work.

I relaxed back in the chair, and we both laughed. We talked easily for a long time, and then she led me to another office to meet the executive director of adolescent care, and the author of *It's Not About the Horse,* Wyatt Webb. As I shook his hand and smiled at him, and then looked from his eyes to Barbara's, I knew it was no mere coincidence that this was all coming together. I felt that kind of calling deep in myself that I had when I first heard about the program. I also knew beyond doubt that whatever happened here, my life wouldn't be the same after.

Barbara took a couple weeks to get back to me with the final word that the job of working with the kids in the new adolescent care program, teaching riding and assisting with therapy, was mine. Then everything happened quickly. She wanted me to start the very next Monday morning. Because the barn wasn't finished, the horses were stabled at a private barn and Barbara gave me directions there. While we waited for the facility to be ready, we'd use the available trails off that barn, and would work the horses to get acquainted with their personalities—and ours.

"We'll school the horses together," she said. She had already hand-picked her herd of ten therapy horses. We worked them every day. Barbara and I firmed our relationship from the horses' backs, riding them two at a time for an hour each on the local trails, and talking about everything. In the weeks leading up to the barn's readiness, we became well acquainted in this easy, extended conversation. We told our stories and experiences in time to the horses' dry shuffling hooves in the parched red dirt. I was honored to be in the presence of this woman whose life's dream was unfolding and wrapping itself around mine, bringing me along in this work.

Barbara talked about what she wanted her program to look like, what Wyatt expected from her, and what she expected from me. With this facility she wanted to demonstrate that a horse can give a broken kid the chance to open up and try, be born once more, to return to a beginning place and risk living. As she spoke, I imagined how a foal chances everything when it rises up on its stick legs for the very first time, to stand and survive or break and die. She said the kids she had worked with were nearly always willing to take the risk of riding a horse, no matter how big or scary to them, even though they knew they might get hurt. There was something about horses.

As I listened to her, I was sure she was right because that's what I had thought as a child. I wanted to risk the hurt because it meant I could get away and survive. It was worth it to me to take the pain I felt inside and use that hurt like fuel to stand and run.

When Sierra Tucson opened its adolescent care program, it didn't include adults in the therapy sessions that involved horses. Many years would pass before adult programs would bloom in which the rest of us could explore similar therapy regimens with horses. But

Wyatt was ahead of his time. He believed in the program so staunchly that he insisted each adult member of his staff come down to the barn and sample this equine experience. The staff was skeptical: Horses seem large and threatening to many of us, the program was brand new, and Barbara's and Wyatt's expectation that horses had a therapeutic power seemed just too much for some of the staff.

There were a lot of staff members who worked with the kids, but few who were horse people. A few members said that they liked the horses, but were just as clear that they didn't really have any interest in what we were doing with them. Some were counselors, or the "activities" guys—like the one who put up climbing ropes for the kids, or the guy who took the kids out on rugged treks. They all had opinions about what Wyatt and Barbara were doing. Most felt the horse work was just another activity where the kids got to go play.

Beautifully designed, Sierra Tucson was a state-of-the-art facility nestled against the Santa Catalina mountains. It offered amenities that would be the envy of any resort, including an Olympic-sized pool and a climbing wall. It was easy to see the horses as one more opportunity for recreation, instead of integral to a very specialized kind of therapy. But those staff members who tried the process and allowed themselves to accept what these animals might be able to do, or who just let the experience in for its own sake, told Barbara and Wyatt that it made sense. Maybe this part of the program was where the work of getting these kids to open up was most truly going to happen.

How did the work *work*? It seems so simple, now, when I take it apart. To an outsider, it might resemble a camp exercise where we groomed the horses, talked, and laughed. That is until the release began to happen, kid with horse. Then something pure and present occurred. If they could talk, the horses might tell us that their "language"—their body movements and behavior—is mostly about survival and that you have to be truthful. Horses can't bluff. If there's danger, run. If there's grass, whinny, call your friends, and eat. Kids in real pain, who finally let it out to someone who will listen, aren't bluffing either. So pairing the two creatures, kid and horse, to try to converse nonverbally, *was* the work—trying to reach the truth.

At first, Barbara only let me facilitate with her, not run a session completely on my own. The kids would come down to the barn in the morning, five at a time, and we would start by sitting in a circle of hay bales. We waited for the tension to ease so the kids would talk. Barbara would ask them to tell us why they were at Sierra Tucson, and what they needed to do so they could go home. Many of the kids were here through a court order for a juvenile offense, to be rehabilitated; it was a kind of end-of-the-line stop before hard time. Others were troubled by abuse or neglect. Barbara asked them what kinds of things they might want to accomplish before they had visits from parents or case workers. Some talked more easily than others; some radiated tension. They were tough and angry and vulnerable and scared, and not one of them wanted to be here.

When Barbara told the circle it was time to go to the horses, you could feel the anticipation and worry dance like static electricity over the kids. Most of them had never been around horses. The horses, meanwhile, were usually out milling around in a large arena made of metal pipe, just being a herd. Barbara would ask the kids one at a time to pick out a horse that he or she felt drawn to, or who called to them in any way.

So, one at a time, each young person entered the pen. The horses, as soon as they became aware of the human, might amble closer or just as likely, start running around. It depended on that particular child's energy. After the child selected a horse, Barbara would tell the horse's name. That was all that happened at this point; one kid stepped out, and then the next could go in. When you selected a horse, you couldn't remove it from the herd until everyone had chosen. Each kid had the right to choose any horse he or she felt drawn to. So if one child wanted the same horse as another, two kids would have to share the animal. When everyone had picked, we brought the horses out and started grooming.

The simple repetitions of brushing and grooming the horses created neutral energy in which the kids could place and release their thoughts.

We had them tie their horses to the metal pipes of the arena, provided the grooming tools, and instructed them in their use. The kids could enjoy the horses and the rotations of currycomb and brush on the dusty hides in silence, or ask questions, or randomly put some conversation in the air for the other kids to hear. A piece of information about their lives, maybe even a worry. The neutral energy present before their emotions entered the grooming event always felt to me like waiting for a cycle on a washing machine to change. First the cycle fills the machine with water with a steady pouring sound, and then *bam!* The cycle changes to wash. Then agitating and more water pouring, rinsing, and then all of a sudden *bam!* and the gears change the cycle. Like a whirlpool the spin starts slowly and the wild draining begins.

The atmosphere with the kids cycled through stasis and explosion. They would groom and groom, and someone one would erupt suddenly into tears about some particular history of abuse, or pure anger at dropping a brush and looking dumb, or one would cry out from falling headlong into the depths of an emotional landscape.

"No one's ever loved ME. I'm all alone. I hate him. I hate her," they'd say.

And sometimes, connections occurred in unexpected actions, like the girl who groomed Adonis. Adonis was a lunk of a horse, snowy white, overweight and docile as only horses who trust their people and get regular meals and brushings can be. Sue, a dark-haired girl with thick glasses, had chosen Adonis from the herd and tied him by a fraying blue rope at his halter to the arena pipe. She pushed the rubber curry comb around on his back and his barrel in the circular motions I showed her to remove the dead hair and get the blood up to the surface of the horse's skin. She started at the neck, down the sagging back and hefty barrel to the horse's rump. She worked the hair there a long while before tentatively moving her hand down the hind leg, edging closer to the Adonis' underside. Because his barrel was round, she had to bend from her waist to see where her hand was going on the inside of his leg. Horses are one with their bodies always, and respond to the slightest human touch. A hand that smoothes his coat calms him and he'll sometimes inhale deeply, then exhale in relaxation. Adonis, being an untroubled horse at rest, had also let his penis "drop" or extend from his sheath, perfectly enjoying the sensation of being groomed.

As Sue looked under and realized where her hand was headed, near that large penis, her face tightened and she started to cry, turning her face away and out to the aisle. She continued to groom him, but only by feel. Her lips were compressed to a line across her face and she squeezed her eyes shut behind the glasses. She shook as she struggled to finish the grooming.

In a still moment like this, a kind of healing started. Barbara or I would stop the child, and ask questions that could gently open doors to their trouble.

"I see that you're crying; I'm wondering what emotion this has brought up for you?" Barbara inquired, in a structured dialogue meant to be candid but without threat.

Sue wiped her face on her sleeve, leaving a dirt streak behind.

"Just breathe," Barbara said. Adonis swiveled an ear to our voices.

Sue exhaled the words, "I can't."

"It's okay. Take your time."

The girl stood stiffly, biting at the skin on her lower lip. She roughly wiped tears from her face with the back of her hand.

"It's so big," she said.

"What's so big?"

"That," she said. "Just like his. I remember his thing was huge. Not just big. Huge." As the girl told us what she could of her story, we heard that Adonis's penis had ignited a memory of what to a small child being sexually abused seemed giant-sized.

I so resonated with her and knew her story as if it were my own. I walked over to her and put my arm on her back in support. She wept more until her entire body heaved out the tears. The other kids watched in silence. I knew it then—this was my calling—to become part of this facility, to become a mentor and example for these kids, to show them how healing through these horses could be safe. Around the horses, they might feel vulnerable, but the animals would always let them feel and speak whatever came to them. Maybe Sue didn't feel as good about what happened as I did, but I suspected she knew something *had* changed for her.

Barbara was right about the horses. I thought about the kids who would be lucky enough to experience this remarkable care and emotional release. And I made the connection that I was still a kid here, and I desperately wanted to heal. Maybe anything was possible.

My own role started as wrangler or outfitter, as I took the kids on trail rides. I was amazed at the ease I felt with them. I hovered between adult and child myself, and didn't trust either "Shelley" most of the time. But with them, everything seemed okay. Some were tough and wanted to test me first, but I stood up to it. Others hung back and waited for my direction. I gave them a little and invited them to come forward for more. For the rides, we'd all saddle the horses together, with me supervising, and then amble off onto the dusty trail in a straggly group. Because my first concern with these young riders was that we all stayed together, I'd twist in my saddle so that I could face them and talk and watch for any issues with the horses. They laughed at me "riding backwards." About ten minutes into the ride, the trail widened into an open brown field, and the horses relaxed because they could see all the space ahead into the distance. Horses are always looking for that "something" that means danger. To see a space free of trees and open to the horizon meant "no lions today." The kids liked the openness too—they could see every adult who might be coming.

As we rode, the kids told me stories about the notches and gashes in their lives. I absorbed how much they'd already gone through, young as they were. I watched as they agreed with someone whose voice partnered their own. Under that bowl of blue sky, on a dry field, they sought a kind of comfort from each other. As we rode, the tension lifted. No longer was it just one of them, alone and fighting. They had other kids here who would listen and acknowledge their life experiences. Speaking to one another began their opening, and for some, their healing. And the horses? They were witnesses, ears cupped to the voices and stories.

By the end of the afternoon, with the sun melting across the trail, I felt gratitude, to be with my own kind, both horse and struggling human. As I got more comfortable in my position at Sierra Tucson, Barbara gave me more leeway with the kids. She saw the relationships developing among them with me, how they trusted me. I was closer to their age than Wyatt or Barbara or their counselors. I was in my early thirties, and ready to talk to them about anything. In reality, I was still close to the start of my own recovery from what I call "co-dependency in relationships." I'd had just a few years, give or take, in therapy working on trying to remove my need to be in control and to manipulate my relationships, and not allowing that to be done to me. As a legacy of my abuse, this was never easy. I had spent thirty days in rehab for this at its most extreme a couple years earlier to find my center. Now in Tucson, I wanted a group to belong to.

Because I would listen to them, these kids gave me trust. Finding a good listener was hard for them. They weren't used to it, and it was rare for them to be heard by a counselor or parole officer without their having to consider what "points" it might make or lose for them. With me, and with Barbara, they were able to express themselves. I was sustained by their acceptance and need.

I wasn't scheduled to work on the weekends. So when the phone rang that Sunday morning, I was watering a lemon tree in my yard. When I answered, Barbara was level and clear and told me one of the youngest kids, Erik, had run away from Sierra Tucson. No one could find him. Everyone was looking, the police included. Did I know anything about where he might be? Had he said anything to me?

I told her the truth—I had no idea. But I would drop everything and come in and look. Barbara said no, they were doing what they could. Hopefully he would turn up by nightfall—someone had to know where he was.

On Monday morning, with Erik still gone, Wyatt called the staff to confer about the search. A staff member spoke up and said that he thought one of the kids, Amy, seemed pretty tight with Erik. Another staff member agreed. They were sure she would know where he was.

As Wyatt turned to me, every eye in the room followed his lead.

"I'd like you to take Amy on a ride. See if she'll tell you where he is."

I looked back at Wyatt, then at the others.

"I'm willing to do that," I said, feeling like I was being asked to betray my own kind. "But you need to know that I'm going to tell her you asked me to do this. I'm not going to lie to her or bait her into telling me something that she doesn't know or doesn't want to tell. I've got to be truthful with these kids from the start or I'll lose every ounce of trust they've given me."

Wyatt nodded.

I got up and left the room, feeling more like one of the kids than one of the staff.

Within the hour, Amy and I saddled up two horses, Bo, a big chestnut gelding for me, and Snip, a smaller gray gelding for her. We rode off like a posse on the dusty trail from the barn. What happened with her on that ride seemed almost too coincidental and easy, as if it was planned. Now, looking back, I can see the connections I had with these kids and why what felt like my own action—going on that ride—was really as directed by what the kids wanted as by any request of Wyatt's, because they trusted me.

About an hour and half out on the trail, Amy, who had had been fairly quiet, stopped her horse and spoke.

"Are you going to ask me where Erik is?"

I stopped too. "Are you offering me that information?"

"Well I know you brought me out here so I could tell you."

"You're right," I said. "They're all waiting for us to get back there, to see if you told me. I said if you didn't want to tell me, that was your choice. We can just take this trail ride, and go back. But if you want to tell me, if you know where he is, and if we can get Erik back safely, then we should probably head back so we can get your friend home."

Amy reached out her pale arm to my deeply tanned one holding the reins.

"I'm only going to tell you because I know it's the best thing for him. He'll just get in more trouble. He left on foot. He got to the airport and called me. He says he's okay. I don't know where he's going, Shelley, or how he got out there. I really don't."

Amy paused and then turned in her saddle to face me.

"Telling you guys the truth all the time is really hard," she said. "Erik says it bugs him. I think he's really scared. He told me he runs away when he's scared."

I nodded and kept quiet. Feeling frightened is intricately tied to this work of telling the truth to yourself. I don't know anyone who is sincere about this work that doesn't experience times that are pure black, utterly lonely, and packed with certainty that no matter what you say, someone else will see how broken you are inside. The kids could easily think that those who were seemingly so "well" like me, or not sent here by parents or the court, only listened because they had to. Maybe those of us on the staff were judging them. Maybe we were waiting for them to give us a signal that they were strong and trustworthy enough now that we could turn our attention to someone else.

I wanted something more for them. I believed my behavior around them, and respect for their need to tell or not, whatever their story might be, could show them that I wasn't going to pass a "ruling" on their life if they shared what mattered with me.

So Amy and I rode back, put the horses away, and walked into Wyatt's office. With my arm around her for reassurance, I told Wyatt that Erik was at the airport. When the staff got there, Erik seemed relieved to be found. Sometimes we send up a flag for help without realizing it.

Erik spent time in solitary for leaving, confined to his room and eating alone for about a week. The counselors tried to justify to the rest of the kids what happened with Amy's outing of Erik's whereabouts to me, as if it was a validating experience for everyone. We all learned something from this. But the kids knew what we were doing: covering up the fact that they'd missed Erik slipping out with this story of "a good experience of trusting us enough to protect one of our own from harm." But it seemed to me that if we just told them the truth, like Amy knew she could get from me, then it didn't matter that they were onto us, or that we counselors would feel better about what happened if we gave the story a larger meaning. We could still get the information we needed, and no one lost face or respect. On the other hand, if you skated around or lied or tricked them as had happened so often in their lives, they weren't going to tell you a thing. You could make up your own truth and tell that story over and over until you were blue in the face.

Maybe we hang on to the feelings from something that hurt us because we've learned to lean into the pain for an awkward kind of support. Even though it hurts, we're used to it, it belongs to us, and so we keep it around. Horses do this. I've met so many kind, never-grumpy animals who are "cinchy," meaning they don't like it when you tighten their saddles, no matter how slow or careful you are, and pin their ears or turn their nose to you as if to say "I'll bite that hand if you keep it up." Others are ear-shy and won't let you touch one ear, though whatever originally happened to that ear is several owners back. Horses don't seem to forget, but will change their behavior if you're consistent in what you ask of them, and how. Is this behavior change a result of learning human language? Or a way of respecting our request? Regardless, it is surely an attempt to communicate with us.

Telling the truth to yourself, despite your pain, was the foundation of the work at Sierra Tucson. The kids knew the truth about their issues, and we certainly weren't the first to listen carefully and honorably. Still they leaned into the pain. But by introducing the horses to experience the kids' feelings in telling true things, both creatures made a stab at living with it for that day. It was a start forward. Each horse responded to a story's energy—or the lack of it, if you weren't present and focused in telling it. The kids responded to the big animals' constant body warmth and presence, and total inability to pass a judgment on them.

Steven can tell this story for me. A young African American with one perfect right leg and the left lost at mid-thigh, he wore a prosthetic limb. He came to the program as a last resort on court order, with a history of increasingly less-than-petty crimes. I knew his case history mentioned an abusive father, but I didn't know details. The kids knew the leg was fake, even if Steven limped only a little. They asked baldly, "Hey Steven. What's with the leg?" He wouldn't be caught without it, but I did see him early one morning through the screen door to his room, balanced on his one good leg like a dark crane. I imagined that bum leg made it hard for him to be cool. But when he turned to look at me, I couldn't prove it.

Steven didn't waste words, almost as if they were expensive, and getting them right cost him. On a morning that started fresh but would turn furnace-like, he had come down to the barn and announced he wanted to ride Vargas.

Vargas' history was that he belonged to Barbara, but Wyatt resonated with him in an unmistakable way. At seventeen hands Vargas was a giant to the kids, a light bay nearing buckskin Dutch Warmblood. When Barbara first brought him into the program, Wyatt hadn't spent a lot of time learning to ride, so Barbara and I both spent time getting him familiar with Vargas. Watching her work, it seemed to me as if Barbara offered Wyatt some secret about how he could get into that horse's heart. She showed him how to communicate with Vargas through touch and smell and emotion. Wyatt and the horse formed a tight bond.

Like Vargas, Wyatt had formed a bond with Steven, and specifically asked to be notified if Steven asked to do something that could get him in trouble. Wyatt wanted Steven to succeed here because the stakes were very high.

"You'll have to ask Wyatt if you can ride him," I said to Steven.

"No problem," Steven answered in his casual way. He turned on his heel and walked back to the office to get Wyatt's approval, that slight limp giving him a certain steely dignity. He could have been a young cowboy, injured in some chore, walking back to the bunkhouse.

Wyatt returned with him.

"Wyatt wants to help me groom him," Steven said. "I said that's okay, but I don't need the help. Wants to watch me, I guess."

Vargas snorted, resting a back leg and standing on three. He accepted the grooming like it was his due.

"I like this guy, that's all," Wyatt said, covering who he meant by "this guy," horse or boy, with his offhand statement. "I check in on Shelley occasionally to see how the horses are doing. You'd both better take good care of this one."

Wyatt looked directly to me.

Steven stroked with the brush until Vargas shone like molten caramel. Wyatt waited until Steven moved around to Vargas' tail, and then patted Steven's shoulder.

"Good job. He's all yours. Take it easy out there."

I thanked Wyatt as he left, and turned my attention to Steven as he saddled Vargas. By this time, Barbara had arrived and stood hands on hips. Steven slapped the saddle pad in place and went to get the rest of his tack.

"You know," I said to Barbara, "you should ask Steven take off that prosthesis before he rides. He won't be able to balance on Vargas because he's so wide-backed, and Steven will push on his real leg without balancing on the other leg. He'll fall for sure."

"He's more comfortable with both legs," she said. "His choice, and he wants to wear it."

"But if he doesn't have the false security of that leg in the stirrup, he'll be able to balance himself naturally, on his seat bones."

Barbara sighed. "We can't humiliate him like that, asking him to take his leg off, even if we know what might happen. We're here to watch and let him take the initiative."

"But everyone knows that leg isn't going to help him ride, and we know we're supposed to know better than the kids about safety. Let's think about what's going to happen."

"No," she said, as Steven slipped the bridle over Vargas' head. "He has choices. If that leg feels right to wear, that's where we'll go with him."

He turned to look at us, smart enough to know we were talking about him. He led Vargas to the mounting block and got up. Steven started at a walk in the ring, and I talked to him about relaxing as much as he could in the saddle.

"You look stiff."

"You're the stiff one," he said back. "I'm fine."

I didn't get my hint across, or maybe like some of the kids, he wanted to show me what he could really do. He started to trot. His balance changed, imperceptible to anyone but the horse and me. As Vargas sensed the shift, he moved faster to catch himself up under the boy's center of balance. Soon Vargas broke into a gentle canter. Steven tried to ride on both legs but succeeded only on his real one, tipped wrong in the saddle, and caught his bad leg at a bad angle in the stirrup. The prosthesis came off his leg as if it were a loose shoe and fell to the dirt.

Vargas saw a limb appear out of thin air. He might have thought that the leg on the ground was his own leg come loose, or the human's leg. And if it was the human's, where the hell was the rest of him? Vargas blew and shied, then started bucking for his life. Steven lost all grip and fell. When Vargas saw the body join the leg on the ground, but apart from each other, he pounded away to the far end of the arena to stand snorting and trembling.

Steven sat up in the dirt and raised his hand to me, like a bronc rider pitched off before the eight-second limit to let the crowd know he was okay. He brushed the dust off his arms and good leg. Barbara and I got him up, then she went to call the doctor down from the center. Everything checked out fine, nothing broken. Steven took the false leg from the doctor and handed it over to me.

"I want to try again. You keep this."

None of this should have happened, but you never would have been able to convince Steven until he experienced it himself. If we told Steven the truth that he had to learn to ride with that one good leg before he could ride with one real and the other a prosthetic limb, he might not have fallen. Of course he could ride with a false leg, but he needed to learn his center and balance first, and he would have to teach that to his body before he could teach it to his leg. Truth is a dead-center thing.

Steven's fall taught me that I, too, needed to stay true and honest to myself, and to try to be heard, even if those listening didn't want to hear me. Talking until I feel I am heard is hard; the human language isn't precise and you have to use a lot of words sometimes to get the communication right. It's easier for me to go quiet. I doubt my worth to be heard. But staying silent makes for an awkward safety. As my grandfather said, "If you tell, you will die." He didn't mean he would kill me, but he knew if I told what was really going on I would have to take the scrutiny and face the disbelief because I was a kid. In a sense what I thought of as "me" would die. In this incident, when I didn't insist to Barbara or tell the truth directly to Steven, Steven got hurt. Someone usually does.

Truth or consequences, the saying goes. Eight months after I was hired in the horse program at Sierra Tucson, I was fired for not telling the truth.

In my application, I told Sierra Tucson that I had graduated from college, but I hadn't. From research I've done as an adult, from going to therapy, and from watching and thinking about my own behavior, I know this clearly: adult survivors of sexual abuse just like me often sabotage their own work and prosperity. If I had told the truth and argued for my skills and professional horse knowledge, I might have been hired on anyway. But I didn't. Finally, I had landed the perfect job, suited to my life experience and recovery. I loved this work and was devoted to the kids and the horses and Barbara and Wyatt. But because I lied, they let me go. Barbara and Wyatt were sorry, but they had clear rules, and the institution's policies applied to everyone. How could this program have any credibility with the kids if the staff wasn't honest? Who would they believe?

From that beautiful facility, I set out like a prodigal daughter in search of what my life could be. I found a riding program outside of town that presented itself as a therapy program, but Sierra Tucson and this place only had horses in common. The owner and "program director" here wanted me to train his herd into therapy horses that he could use constantly in a string of rides. This protocol didn't match Sierra Tucson at all in depth or care. I transitioned from the most peaceful, loving place and job to this hell, and I believed I deserved it. If you tell, you die, but if you go on living a lie, are you living?

At the new job, I worked seven Arabian horses, all smaller than those in the Sierra Tucson herd. The owner didn't choose these animals for the work they would have to do, and the horses didn't know how to do the jobs they were picked for. Because the client unloads an incredible amount of emotional baggage onto the horse, and the horse absorbs all that energy, a therapy horse has a very difficult and strenuous role. He needs time off, to have a break between clients. In a good, basic therapeutic riding program (and Sierra Tucson followed this model), the therapy horses worked six months and got six months off, or worked three and got three off. The horses got time to recover from the strain of work with troubled humans. Rotating horses like this, into and out of therapy, enables them to come back on fresh and relaxed, much the way we refresh ourselves when we go on vacation.

I tried to do the best I could with his herd, until the day a few months later when the owner "acclimated" a new horse to the round pen used for facilitated riding therapy by running the little gelding around inside it until he nearly dropped. The horse wasn't used to a round pen, or to having humans handle him nonstop, and he had been taking off at a run as soon as he was let loose in the pen. This time the owner ran him and ran him, cracking a whip at the horse's flank to keep him moving. After more time than I care to remember, the horse stopped dead, and hung its head, sides heaving in and out. It didn't matter if the round pen was scary. His dull eye showed he no longer cared about where he was at all. The owner came in and slapped the horse on the rump without getting a flinch.

"He won't be running from much now," he said.

The horse seemed to know what the human words meant. *Give in.* And right then I swear that dull look in his brown eye changed and I saw *No.*

I heard the horse, listened to him, and left. I couldn't give in either.

It's late afternoon at my riding lesson with Sabina, and still raining. The metal roof sheds water in sheets. The pounding reverberating through the indoor arena sounds like the end of the world. Only three riders endure the downpour with their mounts. Two are leaving. I sidle up to Sabina at the mounting block and ask how it went this week.

"I just get so frustrated. It's not working," Sabina says.

Sabina is in her early forties and Innis is ten. Even with me, a different trainer, the pair still struggle to relax into movement. Horses move forward naturally, the urge to *keep* moving so very strong and survival-driven. So when I see one holding back, and if she's not lazy by nature, I know something's wrong. The rearing behavior set this pair back, but we worked through most of the cause, which was Sabina restraining Innis through a tight seat and anxious hands. I don't think Sabina trusts herself to tell Innis the truth and just let her know she's still worried about riding her, for all the reasons a forty-something woman would worry. Sabina fears the bigger movement, falling off and getting hurt, and the specter of the rearing behavior returning. This isn't easy.

I can also see that Innis worries about her own place in Sabina's herd. She might be wondering if Sabina is in charge, or does she want Innis to be? The mare's jaw and back are tight, and she's stiff under her rider. On the surface, this really isn't a terrible pair. But what lies beneath the pair is serious. Lack of trust. I see how they can solve this, and I can show them. But until Sabina asks me directly, or attempts to look at the truth of what she fears, I can only guide, not solve. This isn't a training issue; this is a lack of belief in herself that comes through in the language of horse as "*I can't move.*" And so Innis cannot become Sabina's partner because Innis moves to *live*. Sabina is a liability.

"Show me what's up," I say.

I can talk to Sabina, but I'm always safer watching and then showing. I have a hard time getting the human language right. Rounding the arena, I see the same stiffness in horse and rider. Sabina asked me if a different bit might help, or a chiropractor that someone in the barn has recommended for Innis. I've answered her questions with "maybes." She knows those won't work.

"Ask her to stretch," I say.

"She won't," clearly irritated with me, herself, and Innis.

"Come on. Try."

"I am."

I watch the pair resisting each other. Sabina stops Innis and walks her to me.

"This isn't any better at all. I hate this. She hates me."

"That's a human emotion," I say. "What's bugging you?"

"Bugging me?"

"Do you want to quit?"

"Well, do you see what's wrong?"

"Can you *feel* what's wrong?" I ask.

"I don't know. Do you want to ride her?"

"Are you asking me to ride her?"

Sabina is out of the saddle before I finish my question. She hands me the reins.

So I lead Innis back to the mounting block. First at the walk, I ask her only to stretch her nose out and down toward the dirt. I want her to relax and begin to lift her back under the saddle, to chew the bit. At the trot, I ask for the same but with more energy. She samples me as a new rider, and tries to hollow herself and avoid relaxing. But she also senses that my seat and hands are different, that they offer her no hurt or worry, and after several circles, she is getting a message about a new partnering.

"Of course she'd do it for you," Sabina remarks.

I ask Innis to slow down, and then walk beside Sabina.

"Why do say that?" I ask.

Sabina drags her boot in the dirt. When she looks up, her face is so tired.

"I wish I could trust her," she says.

"What does trust feel like? I'm not trying to make you mad—I really want to know. And Innis needs to know. What's going on? What in this belongs to Innis?"

She pauses, and then reaches out to stroke the mare's neck.

"I'm scared I can't ride her."

"Innis feels that," I say. "So mount up, and tell her it's your deal that you don't trust her."

"I do like her. She's a good mare."

"Right. But she's worried."

"She's worried? And so I'm a chicken?"

"Is that the truth?"

Sabina takes the reins from me in response, sighs, and mounts up.

"No, but neither of us is very brave," she says. "Why can't she be brave for me, so I'll trust her? I want her to show me first."

Now we are closer to something real.

I say, "Think about telling her in your head, as you ride, what you need from her."

Horses feel everything you offer them—you're on their back, in the place they are most vulnerable, and they have to be prepared to respond. They're hard-wired to listen to muscle and breath and emotion, almost as if they can feel what's in your head. Sabina inhales deeply and sits up straighter.

"Keep her thinking about you. What would it be like to be brave for her first?"

Sabina and Innis make small circles that get a little more trusting, then they move out to larger ones, until finally, in just the last couple strides, Sabina feels the result I got in the saddle. Innis stretches long and low and chews on her bit. Sabina looks over to me for confirmation.

"Did you tell her something true?" I ask.

Sabina doesn't need to answer. Innis snorts that long kind of blowing breath that means to me, "I accept, I understood, and it felt okay."

Barbara Rector owns my deepest admiration for causing the phenomenon of psychotherapy on horseback to achieve reality. Around the world other people have started programs, but Sierra Tucson Adolescent Care, under Barbara Rector and Wyatt Webb, became the first accredited facility to offer the therapy. The field is still so wide open, and many people are diving in and out with varying levels of offerings, success, and accreditation. I have a clear sense, however, that there is an inventor of the way to learn human as a second language—an equine Dr. Doolittle—it is Barbara. For those of us whose first "language" is something akin to primitive communication through instinct and image and body and reaction—through the language *under* words—we can be given a chance to learn to speak with our own kind through a program that uses horses as teachers, like Sierra Tucson.

But even true fairy tales end. Sierra Tucson closed its therapeutic riding program two years after it opened. The costs were high, and not enough private participants were enrolled or covered by insurance to make it viable. Public dollars and support only went so far.

You can now find Barbara doing her work through a program called Adventures in Awareness in Arizona. I think about her often when I teach, or hear about a troubled kid who could benefit from the chance to work with a horse. When I am training a horse for a rider, and listening to the horse, I want so badly to be able to translate purely how the horse can communicate with me, so that I can relay it in "human" to my own kind, with the horse's truth and clarity.

I'm done with Sabina's lesson, and I stuff her check into the pocket of my breeches. She leads Innis back down the aisle to her stall. I think the trust issue they are working through will surface again, as it must until they become fluent in the comfort of each other and their ability to talk in the language of body and heart. Most especially heart. I'm hopeful for them. Sabina has now experienced *the thing that means safety* in "horse," and Innis has understood the meaning of *the thing that means trust* in "human."

I've got to head home and drag my water-logged arena, clean stalls, and do the evening feed. As I maneuver my white, one-ton pickup truck through the narrow gate and onto the road, I want music, turn on my radio, and seek something familiar. I land on a Spanish station. Even after so many years in Arizona, I can't speak this language, but I can feel the sad sweetness of the song circling me in the cab. Maybe the song is about love. I trust that it is.

5
Full Pirouette

Cowboy is a thirty-one year old brown Quarter Horse who simply lives on my place, no longer worked. He belongs to a client of mine who wants him to have a retirement in which he can wander about, not confined to a small stall, and just enjoy being. Cowboy does that—sampling my supply of alfalfa one minute, entering the tack room the next to see if the grain buckets are open and accessible, and sometimes poking into my backyard and circling the above-ground pool, leaving a manure pile near the orange tree as his calling card. Because of his extreme age, I worry about every turn in his behavior. He is a horse in slow motion, sliding through air, chewing for eternity, his hair overly curly and long because his system doesn't work the way it used to. I have to clip him regularly to keep him comfortable in the Arizona heat.

One morning recently, I came into the barn early, my boxer, Boboli, at my side. It wasn't a good day for Cowboy, and he was listless. My thermometer confirmed he was running a temperature. With this antique horse, I looked for that change of season in his eye that meant *I'm too tired to face this day, let me go.* I had no idea if this would be his day to go, but I called the vet anyway to do whatever could be done. I am his voice if he's in trouble and needs an advocate, even for an ending.

While I waited on hold for the vet, I thought about Cowboy, and this image of the old horse shifted into one of what he must have been like young. I could see him small and brown, maybe standing lonely at a fenceline calling to his mother who is far off in the pasture. He might have felt helpless—he can see her, but he is little and she is very distant. In this daydream, I call to him, *Cowboy,* and point toward his mother with encouragement. He whinnies his understanding, and tries to scrabble off on his spindly legs. Someone has to speak for you and remind you of the way when you feel lost.

When the vet answered, I told her about Cowboy.

"Keep him quiet. I'm leaving for my rounds and can stop by in a bit."

I closed my cell phone, and thinking about my day ahead, realized too late that I couldn't be here for the vet. This was the day I was taking my mother in for her gall bladder surgery. More worry clouded my morning, this time about her going under anesthesia. I knew I'd be there all day. She's in her seventies, and though this was a routine surgery, I wasn't ready for her health to take a turn for any reason. I opened my phone again and called my horse sitter to wait for the vet instead of me. The more I thought, the more anxious I was becoming. Where was this feeling rising from? My daydream returned and I saw Cowboy as a foal again. He stands at my bedside. I'm very young here and the dark in the room is ebony and moonless. Cowboy puts a whiskered, velvet nose to my shoulder, the best kiss from a horse. We both startle and raise our heads because we hear my Grandfather's footsteps traveling the dream's hallway to our door. Cowboy tells me, *run somewhere to safety as fast as you can.* But I'm lost and scared. *I can't,* I mumble, and throw my arms around the foal's neck to bury my face in the sweetness of his warm hide.

Boboli nudged my hand with his snout. Like vapor, the daydream lifted to return me to the barn. I broke into tears suddenly, thinking of being young and lost. Crying for myself that on this day, I would take care of my mother, but would not feel cared for myself. Something ached in my chest.

Silence is a real dimension, like time or space, but its air is thick and still like amber. You can enter here by choice, by accident, or through trauma. In this dimension, everything looks familiar and nearly real, until you sense with a growing horror that in this plane you have no mouth and cannot speak. Where your lips once smiled, now there is just a flat space of skin like a mask.

I was originally sent here by the shame caused by my grandfather's abuse. I was twenty-four years old when my grandfather finally died, and until he passed, my brother Ron and I lived in the silence of what occurred, and the sureness that if we told anyone what happened, our grandfather would get revenge. It took me three more years before I could even try to form words around my story for my first therapist. But a story always seeks a listener. In the mid-1980s, I found just enough energy to struggle to the surface of myself because I knew if I didn't, I wouldn't ever get better. My relationships had suffered, and I had no clue how to be myself. I needed to rebuild something to live on.

At about the same time, my mother had come out from Michigan to Tucson to visit with me. I felt stronger than I had in a long while, and my mother and I were getting along better than usual. We both worked to keep our relationship skimming the surface of things. Somewhere in my teens, I got angry with her and couldn't express the reason, and she never probed to determine a cause.

On an ordinary day during her visit, we were shopping in a large store. We talked as we wandered the aisles about items we needed to find, and where we might be going for lunch.

Then without warning, the conversation turned.

"Oh my god, Shelley, I just remembered that I've got to tell you something that's so terrible. Marcia told my sister that Grandpa sexually abused her. Now can you believe that?"

Marcia, my cousin, was close to my age. My heart, like a bird hitting a window, folded in on itself and then re-inflated, startled and torn. Until the moment that my mother mentioned this, I really believed that I would never, ever ruin my mother's life by telling her what her father had done to me. But now, as I felt a channel rip open in the silence, I wanted to swim the thick current and finally try to breathe. I knew I couldn't hide my own truth any longer. If I kept my own story untold, my cousin would be seen as a liar.

I inhaled deeply, and turned to face my mother.

"It's true. The same thing happened to me."

In a single moment, the sound drained out of the day. Nothing existed in space but our two faces, searching each other's eyes for affirmation or reprieve. Then just as suddenly, every noise in the store backfilled my head with static—the announcer telling of a special, the whine of a toddler wanting attention from her mother, the shriek of a wheel on a shopping cart.

My mother stood motionless, my words hanging in air. She suddenly dumped the items she had in her arms into our cart and rushed to the front of the store and out. I followed her to my Jeep. She kept her face turned to the passenger door window and wouldn't speak, and we drove back to my house encased in silence.

On the back porch, before she could pull open the door and vanish into the house, I spoke to her.

"Listen to me. I'll give you one hour of answers to any questions you have about what happened. After that, we won't speak about it again unless I bring it up first."

I desperately needed to control the terms for discussion. As much as this story needed telling, it was so entwined with my life that if I let go of the rules of the telling, I could lose myself in the memory. I didn't ever want my mother to bring it up and surprise me. I was willing to talk about it for that hour, and if *I* brought it up again, I would let her ask about it again.

She turned without answering me and entered the house. I followed. I sat down and waited for her to take the invitation to ask me about what happened.

It took a few moments before she asked her first question. It surprised me more than anything I could imagine her saying.

"Do you think it happened to me?" she said.

And during the next hour, she continued to ask me questions about it in terms of herself and her possible experiences.

On and on and on she talked. How this could be? She didn't ask me specifically about what had happened to me, and she didn't seem to want to explore any details that I remembered about the abuse. It would be several years later, after much more of my own therapy, that I would remember thinking to myself that it probably *had* happened to her, but that wasn't what this particular exchange was about. I would realize that I was truly offering my past to validate and protect

Marcia's integrity. My mother's words of disbelief in the store, if unchallenged, left Marcia standing alone. Maybe when my mother realized that Marcia was telling the truth, because it had happened to her own daughter, she had felt a pain so great that she couldn't ask me about details. Maybe. In the moment at hand, I ached to be heard. But my energy to argue about or explain my past ebbed, and silence swallowed up my words.

My story lived immobilized in amber for nearly ten years and ate away at both my mother and me. We didn't talk again about Marcia's or my experiences in any way—until Marcia called it all back out by letting us know she was coming for a visit.

It was now the mid-1990s, and my mother had moved from Michigan to Tucson. After a series of incidents that convinced us both her Tucson neighborhood was becoming increasingly crime-ridden, and not a place I wanted my mother to be, I'd built a small guest house on my property that she rented from me.

Marcia's call enabled my mother and me to have a common ground to reconnect. We were both excited to have her visit after so many years. Because I don't cook, didn't care for my mother's cooking, and wanted to show my cousin some of Tucson, we agreed to take Marcia out to dinner.

The restaurant we picked was shady inside, a cool respite to the evening heat. The waiter brought us margaritas, and Marcia and I, glad to see each other, fell into immediate conversation, talking about everything. It didn't take long for the subject of our grandfather to surface. She wanted to talk about it, and I wanted to share what I knew and had experienced. Before long, it seemed, two hours had passed, and my mother had sat through the dinner in polite silence while we went over the whole of what we both remembered. Until I listened to Marcia echoing my own past, I had refused to believe it was possible that my grandmother, much less my mother, could have known what my grandfather was doing and not tried to stop it. How could an adult woman not want to rescue a child-woman? Surely we would reach out and protect our own kind. I wanted to believe that my grandmother was innocent of the entire thing. But as Marcia's words sank in below my skin, settling next to my heart, I knew there really was no way she could have been. When my brother and I, or Marcia, or whoever of my family's grandchildren visited, we slept in the room next to my grandfather and grandmother. In that shameful night landscape, we were not utterly silent. We moaned and struggled, but my grandfather was insistent and serious about his business, and you didn't give him "no" without consequence. So we gave in.

As I sipped my third margarita and looked from Marcia to my mother, I imagined a picture. My grandmother reaches into her nightstand for a well-used pair of ear plugs, curls her hair methodically behind each ear. She might stuff in the left plug first, and then the right. As she settles into her pillow, she thinks, guiltily, that she will sleep for this night at least, because one of us—not her—is under his weight.

My mother nursed her drink through a small straw and sat silent, her eyes scanning our two faces. She held her face pleasant and unreadable. I blessed her in that moment for not seeming to judge us or shame us at the table for what we had to go through to open ourselves and tell each other. The details were sordid and the pain still fresh. But Marcia and I needed that interaction and conversation to see that we both had survived. I took in that Marcia had moved on in her life, as best she could. I told her about my plans to write this book to try and heal, that hopefully I might help someone else, somewhere, through the stories. I offered how horses had made it possible for me to go on, and what the animals themselves brought in their strength and steadiness to remedy my breakage. Marcia was excited for the book, relieved that it would validate experiences we'd both had, and joyful that it would bring us together again. When we left that night, we promised to share the future with each other as it unfolded.

My mother kept her quiet distance.

My mother was clearly anxious as we arrived at the hospital, checked in, and got her settled. I was only allowed to stay with her until the staff took her in for prep. I was honestly relieved to have that permission to bolt. I don't like hospitals. I've passed enough time in them with broken bones or to sew up torn pieces of myself from horse injuries. Worse, my keen sense of smell overwhelmed me with odors way too sharp and antiseptic.

My mother sought my hand with hers and squeezed it tight. It felt strange, having her hold on to me like that. I didn't want the responsibility of taking care of her after the surgery, I admit it, but I was the one person available. My brother was too far away in Michigan, and while she has friends, she is, after all, my mother. Of course I want her to be well, and I want to be able to love her in a way that will matter to both of us. But when I have to take care of her in this manner, when she is so vulnerable, I am angry and almost can't. I think she feels that way too. I can attribute some of what I experience to being a certain kind of daughter—some like me strike hard to create distance from our mothers so that we can take risks and stretch and leave. In my case, I also know my blue-white anger represents me crying, small and young, *you didn't help me,* and wishing beyond hope that even now she might finally see me for who I am and what I've gone through. I want her to acknowledge it and make it right.

Of course, she can't. She's a daughter too, perhaps one who knew what her mother knew, or experienced something like I did, just long forgotten.

Here in the hospital we had switched places, and in the role of mother, I was just scared I'd lose her completely.

The surgery went as expected with no complications. The vet reached me as I drove us home to say Cowboy might have a tumor in his gut, or it might be old age, but whatever it was, he wasn't thriving. Cowboy was drugged to the gills but still in pain. We talked about other feeding regimens, as he could no longer digest his hay. He easily ate up the grain I gave him, but the truth was he was ancient. After talking to the vet (still driving), I called Cowboy's owner and told her the news. Of course she wanted me to do whatever I could to make it better. I planned to look in on him when I got home. Right now, my mother sat groggy at my side. I could smell the anesthesia metabolizing in her body. She smelled of old age and worry.

At home, I thought if I could just get her into her house, I would be free of my duties for the day, but she softly told me she needed help.

"I can't put on my pajamas by myself."

Of course she couldn't; she'd had surgery and no doubt her abdomen was sore and moving at all hurt like hell. I set down my things. What was I thinking.

"I have to go to the bathroom," she said.

She looked at me with disgust, knowing she didn't want my help or to do this action in front of me, any more than I wanted to see it.

If my anxiety were a red flower, then at the heart of the flower was pure crimson panic. I passionately did not want to take care of someone who had failed to advocate for me. Where I could be present and soft for a horse, where I could try to engage with my clients in a decent way, here in the landscape of my mother I was lost, terrified, and furious.

In the bathroom, assisting her, I felt overcome by the effects of her aging. Her breasts hung flat and heavy, her skin smelled of the antiseptic wash, and she was so small. I took the pair of pajamas from the hook behind the door and slipped the top over her head, and pulled the bottoms up over her legs. She was in pain, and even I could feel it as she moved. I didn't know what to do with it. As soon as I got her settled on the couch, I left her house. Outside I stood just beyond her door and inhaled deeply. The stale hot air was so much fresher than the breath of discovery and shame in my lungs.

"I can't do this." I called a friend to tell her about my mother.

"She's old, Shelley; it's just what you have to do."

"Where was she for me?"

"This is different."

"How?"

"This is surgery. Present day. I know you're hurt, but what you're talking about happened in the past."

"Today it doesn't feel like the past. I don't want to take care of her. I didn't sign up for this."

"She's your mother."

"Yeah, and I repeat, where was she for me?"

"I thought you said you loved her and you were afraid she'd die?"

"I am. I don't understand it either."

I hung up, disgusted with myself.

In the barn, Cowboy rested with his head hung low in the evening sun. His bottom lip drooped and his fly mask, a well-worn blue one, sagged around his ears. I stroked his neck and could tell by touch that his temperature was higher than it should be. His breath was shallow and he didn't move under my hand.

I don't like being the one who's on watch with a dying horse. I've done it enough to know the drill, when to call the vet, when not to intervene, what is required to bury or render the carcass. Endings bring their own silence. The barn after a horse's passing feels out of balance. Some people believe you should let the living members of the herd say a kind of goodbye to the dead friend, either by allowing them to sniff the body, or by leaving the body where they can see it. I think horses are far cannier than that. They likely intuited the passing long before its event. The spirit of the horse is a powerful energy that stirs the leaves on the lemon and orange trees in its wake. Even the cactus stretches its needles to feel the passing. In our human way, we are always surprised and concerned when the turn in health occurs. Standing here with Cowboy I realized what I was avoiding with my mother in her little house: Making a peace with her ending, whether it came today or years from now. Anger is a living thing that breathes life into each action, and only the angry one can extinguish it. To lay it aside and forgive is so hard. Like giving birth to a new self, there is no guarantee that I won't get hurt again and have to survive. The risk seemed too high a price to pay today.

In 2002 I told my mother that I wanted to write this book. She listened but said little for or against the idea. When I had the first chapters in draft, I let her read them. Despite that Marcia and I had talked about this in her presence before, my mother's anger rose fresh and immediate. She didn't speak a word to me for three months.

Telling a story like mine or that of anyone who has been through some form of abuse or life-threatening experience is hard. But when someone who really matters to you refuses to acknowledge that she heard it, you want to somehow retell or rewrite it in a louder voice, with more color and outrage. You want to be *seen* in that story. I didn't go out of my way to ask my mother what her opinions of the book might be or why she became so angry. I knew some of those things in my bones without needing the words. I'd exposed my secret, Marcia's secret, the family secret, and it meant others would now know about it, others who knew my mother. They might ask her, "How could it be that you didn't know?" I wondered if her friends would ask her that, or instead enter the silent dimension to stand guard against the knowledge with her. Her truth against mine. When she did start speaking to me again, she didn't mention the book. I didn't bring it up. Despite my wanting to heal and tell this story, with her I always found myself falling into silence. I couldn't see a way through or out. There is so much we could not talk about together.

I called my mother from my house, which is less than a hundred yards from hers, and asked her how she was doing. We'd been home from the hospital for about four hours. She said she'd like to take a shower, but the doctor told her not to until tomorrow because of the incision. I listened, agreed that that was hard, but I made no offer to bathe her the next day. Instead, I asked if she needed anything from the store, some juice maybe. I told her I'd go out later, after feeding. She responded that she really didn't need the juice, but if I went, then it would be nice.

But I didn't go out. I pulled on my breeches to ride in the cool, early evening, needing release from the day. No matter what else happens in my work day, I ride Laramie, and she's always my first ride. But today, because I had had to take care of Cowboy and my mother, I was very late. She would be my only ride. I saddled quickly, and led her to the mounting block.

A dust devil swirled over the footing in my arena, stretched tall in the wind and then touched down its pointed tail as if it were a small tornado's funnel. The tail dragged this way and that across the centerline of the arena, and as I entered, I watched it dance with the breeze. With a shift in the current, it rose and magically vanished. I walked Laramie to the very place it left earth and found an almost perfect spiral there, like a conch shell cut open to reveal the hidden inner chambers. I didn't walk through it because somehow it seemed sacred or brought to this place for a reason. I seek signs in my life. Guideposts for what to do, where to find help. I could use the direction to find a way out of the emptiness I felt.

After warming up, I asked Laramie to canter and began a small circle. Sitting deeper, I collected and collected until she dropped lower on her hind end and began to slow into a canter pirouette. She didn't stop her canter, but shortened her strides and shifted her balance back on her haunches to move around only the center point of an extremely tight circle. I could almost feel her becoming still under me, yet striding around that perfect shape. I didn't ask for too much of this movement before I took her back out on a larger circle. We had practiced this pirouette just a few strides at a time, day after day, until we reached this near completion of a dance on a still point.

As she finished a stride and I asked her to walk, I remembered the shell pattern in the dust. This full pirouette is like the center where the chambers in the shell spiral to a single point and seem to end. But even in thinking of that spiral, my mind's eye and the canter movement take me from the center point right back to the outer chamber and I must follow it to the point again and again, never ending.

When I put Laramie away, I returned to the arena to look at the spiral one more time, but the wind had erased all trace of it.

I slid open the door to Cowboy's stall. It was late at night, and I came out to be sure he was upright. He looked much better under the barn lights. I knew he'd skated past disaster this time, whatever the cause of his discomfort.

"You've got more luck than most, old man," I said.

Cowboy chewed and put his nose to my shoulder. I led him by the fabric of his fly mask out into the aisle and then to one of the outside paddocks. He'd spend the hours until morning under stars, moving whichever way felt right for him. When I turned back to the barn, I saw the lights were still on in my mother's house. She likely wondered if I would come by. I knew I wouldn't.

The next day I'd help her bathe, and get her some groceries. As the weeks passed we'd both forget this opportunity for intimacy between us, and be relieved just to go on.

When I was very small, my grandfather used my mouth for his pleasure. When I was old enough to contain him, I rested under his weight and endured him. How could the ones who cared for me not know or not act when they knew this man entered the bedroom of the family grandchildren, visit after visit? From the time they were tiny until young adults?

Maybe I'm not ready for this healing work, because I'm not able to forgive my mother when there are others who have hurt me more directly in my adult life, and who I forgive with ease, time and again. No horse I've worked with can offer me solace or a way out of this personal spiral. I can't look any more closely at it than I have. This pain is a scar that healed wrong. I can only tell the story as it is, broken, unfixed, and hard.

If I could, I would write an ending to the story of telling my mother in which we pause in quiet understanding, without movement, and simply care about each other. Perhaps we'd never speak more words about it, but we would be accepting of our different experiences, worries, and justifications. However, that story wouldn't be true. We can't be this way with each other. We spiral in and out of willingness to touch that pain. We want to love each other in the way a mother and daughter can only in dreams. A foal ravaged by a stallion or gelding in a herd would be watched over and mourned by its dam and aunts. Human mothers and daughters are more complex and difficult in their love for each other.

Like the strides of the pirouette, I think that my mother and I circle the point, the very reason we must understand each other. We know the solace available to us if we can perfect and hear the truth between us. The question is how long, at her age and mine, we are willing to practice the movements, or endure the silence, to achieve a peace in which to listen.

6
Two Tracks

My barn and training facility in Tucson occupy five level acres of desert. Four seasons a year, I rise before the sun, groom horses, and begin to train. In the heat season, I start to ride at 4 a.m., and finish the morning at 11 a.m. I resume riding in the late afternoon when the sun gives up on burning a hole through my helmet and turning my arena sand to glass. The winter, and riding in it, is a blessing.

Over many years of working with horses, learning to ride and train them, being a student in barns, and having students in my own barn, I've seen a wide range of horsemanship and horse handling. It's fairly common to encounter the opinion that horses don't have the intelligence we do, and that dominance is the only method of true control.

"They're bigger than us, you know. They can hurt us if we don't keep our guard up."

It's so often about who's in charge.

Sometimes, the events I've witnessed in my years with horses have cried for my intervention. Abuse, in horses and in humans, can be overt or subtle. And horses, like humans, can respond differently to each type. A very sensitive horse can be overcorrected or mistreated once too often and start to deteriorate mentally, doubting itself more and more, its behavior fine-tuning itself to the demands of the rider or trainer until something snaps—call it mind, heart, or will. By whatever name, the horse isn't the same.

In my own therapy work, I've struggled to overcome my grandfather's ever-present warning—don't tell, or you'll die. In working with horses, if you see mistreatment and you tell about it, you risk losing the client or offending the trainer you're learning from. In the past, I have watched and been paralyzed with the fear of telling, too much to stop the abuse or mistreatment, or even to confront it.

As I have integrated my own personal healing into my daily work with horses, and as I listened to their bodies' stories, I've grown stronger. I will not tolerate mistreatment of a horse in my barn. Shelley, the adult trainer of horses, thinks clearly and acts as a trainer should. When I feel a horse in my barn is not getting a fair deal, I intervene, much like a mare protecting a foal, or a herd mate protecting one of its own.

I have lost clients, and friends, over my strong and visceral rejection of abuse and clear mistreatment of horses. Not every person sees it my way—as I've said, horses are big. People have only so much control. Or so they think. I've also lost friends over our need to control each other; humans are very strong.

What is present under our human skin that can boil into anger so easily, that we can hit a horse or yank hard on the metal bit in its mouth? Is it the same thing that makes us hurt one another? Maybe. I keep searching to find a pattern.

I train a number of horses a year, and if I'm lucky, I get to train the owners along with the horses, so that they can benefit from the new knowledge the horse has to offer them. Occasionally, a horse I've trained or owned for myself becomes a student's horse. Renaissance was such a horse. She was a Paint-Arabian cross, black and white in color, talented, and always telling a story with her body. She could do the dressage work *for* you, and you somehow always felt you should be grateful that she did. Unless she worked *with* you, and that was always much harder to achieve.

Mares are very different from geldings in spirit and intention. Renaissance would always be a difficult mare to ride; because if you asked for a movement with an incorrect aid, she would most likely give you a movement you didn't want. She was rarely generous with anticipating what you might want. But if you were paying complete attention to her, *and* you gave her *almost* the correct aid, she might become your partner in the movement, even forgiving your ineptness a little. This acceptance of your full attention by a horse, and its response, is a gift. If you'd brought your own stories up to the saddle and weren't listening at all to what Renaissance was telling you, she would be a challenge to ride—for the simple reason that two beings can't talk at the same time and hear one another clearly. Two tracks, dissonant songs.

The most difficult piece of my own recovery from abuse and the behaviors that isolate me from my own kind has been learning to listen to the stories of others. In the desert, you barely hear a whisper before a storm; the wind's breath hardly enough to stir your eyelashes. But wind in any terrain means a change is coming, and by listening for its first sigh, you can prepare yourself for the change. Listening is a similar art and challenge for me. Horses have taught me how to hear through their bodies; their riders have taught me how to listen to the spaces between the words.

Mary, the woman who bought Renaissance, is the story I'll offer of how hard we must try to listen to each other in order to be ready for the most subtle change in our behavior—the moment that means I am ready to *try* for you, to hear your story. Being heard is the first step in being willing to learn anything, especially about how to heal. But you also have to believe you're being heard, even a little bit, so that you don't run over the listener with your need to be heard in just a particular way. The human interaction is what informs us.

I'd asked Mary to leave my barn once. More than a year ago, she had come back. This morning, I rose tense and guarded, listening to the wind sighing around the walls of my house. It would be her first lesson after the show we'd gone to the previous weekend. I tugged on my schooling breeches, and impatiently, tied back my hair. I was rushed and concerned that I'd have barely enough time to ride Laramie before Mary arrived. Two bottles of water under my arm, I opened the door to the thin sunlight and the feeling of already being behind in my day. The wind licked my arms with its dry tongue.

Mary and I had met several years earlier when she and her daughter Emma watched me for a show season to determine if I was a good enough trainer for Emma, and whether I had any horses in my string worth buying. They knew the reputation of my training barn, asked horse people around Tucson about my methods and philosophy with horses, and then finally came to me seeking a horse for Emma.

Emma was a beautiful and natural rider, more ballerina than equestrienne. At the time, Renaissance—a horse I had owned and had sold, but who was for sale again—was winning in third-and fourth-level classes on the Southern Arizona dressage circuit, a significant achievement that meant she was doing something very right for her rider. I connected Mary and Emma with Renaissance. Emma had several pre-purchase rides before Mary bought her, and we all celebrated the magic in the combination of this rider and horse. Mary, Emma, and I had high hopes.

Emma and Renaissance began to train with me, and I took them to the weekend shows during show season. Mary watched her daughter work, and chafed on the sidelines. Because Renaissance's small stature and refinement suited the physiques of both Mary and Emma, petite women, Mary asked if I would also give her lessons on Renaissance, on weekdays when Emma wasn't showing anyway. She desperately wanted to ride, she told me. *Ride like her daughter* is what she didn't say, but what I felt under her words. Still, I didn't check in with Mary to determine if that was the case. We were each riding on separate tracks in our intentions, and headed for collision.

Renaissance was trained far beyond Mary's ability as a rider, and as is true in any new horse-and-rider relationship, the horse doesn't reveal all she knows to a new rider without some effort on the rider's part. The rider needs patience to unlock the animal's skill and secrets by feeling out, body to body, what is happening. Often a certain amount of listening to each other's spirit is also required. A relationship of quality can, and often does, take years to develop with a particular horse. Most of us would grant that time and care to learn about any friend. But if you are driven to compete, or are used to not listening, you might expect immediate results. A recipe for disappointment.

Lesson after lesson Mary struggled with movements that she knew another rider, for example myself or Emma, was easily achieving. Because Renaissance always wanted her own story heard first, and wanted the rider to get engaged quickly, she began to resist Mary in subtle ways. Unwanted behavior took shape—Mary would ask, inappropriately, for something Mary wanted, and Renaissance would *appropriately* resist because the mare didn't feel Mary's request made sense. Renaissance spooked, shied, and hollowed her back, head held high like an angry child. Mary would get mad or scared of the mare and stop listening, and would too often give in, or worse, give up. Having a fine and strong sense of herself as a horse, Renaissance would take this backing down on Mary's part as success—her behavior achieved the goal of the irritating human work stopping. Consequently, ride after ride, she offered more resistance. Mary got angrier. She wanted a fix, a secret from me, on how to make this work out. I coached, but resistance and irritation were silting into our relationship as well.

Patterns. Horses learn them quickly in training, and anticipate them. To keep the horse listening, you have to feel when the pattern has taken hold in a good way, and also when something is breaking that you need to adjust. I've put this horse knowledge to work in my own therapy to put myself back together. I've learned to recognize and anticipate patterns in my behavior. Sometimes, I can only identify a pattern late, by a specific event that indicates the pattern has repeated itself yet again and is close to its ending. Sometimes I can't identify the pattern at all, and it bites me.

Mary's pattern was an impatient need for progress. She informed me that she also wanted to show on Renaissance, not just watch Emma.

"That's fine," I told her. "Showing goes with the territory of training and rating yourself as a rider. But you ride at a lower level than Emma, so you can't compete at Emma's level with Renaissance."

"What does that mean?"

"You can't show the same horse in a higher-level class this weekend and a lower-level class the next."

The horse was supposed to be moving up the levels in training— not circling the rule book.

Mary listened, but she didn't like the rules, so she didn't hear me.

"I still want to show."

"We'll work on that," I said.

Lesson by lesson, Mary's relationship with me as an instructor deteriorated from frustration to rage, directed primarily at Renaissance in the way she treated her. I thought she wanted me to make it easy for her to make success happen by somehow waving my dressage whip like a wand and enabling her to perform the same movements that Emma or I could do on Renaissance. But because she and I weren't listening to each other's intentions, neither of us was learning. I wanted her to pay attention and give Renaissance a chance. She wanted to be a success on a difficult mare without it being hard. We talked about and around our frustration, until finally losing my temper, I wanted badly to lash out. But I didn't want to lose my client. I couldn't afford an empty space in my barn, or a failure with a student. Here my own bad pattern emerged: Just take it all in; better to abuse myself than to examine the cause closely enough to maybe get hurt, but achieve a better result.

As horses sometimes do, Renaissance became a lightning rod for what was unspoken and highly charged between us. Bad results progressed to worse ones, as Mary handled Renaissance aggressively both in the saddle and on the ground.

Remember the warning from my childhood? If you tell, you'll die? The warning still had teeth, even now that I was an adult. I felt hollow and powerless in difficult relationships like this one with Mary, and in response turned the hate inward on myself. My grandfather, long a ghost now, seemed always right behind my shoulder, caressing me into silence, pleased with my inability and weakness to fight back. If you use a tool, like a rake, without gloves, over a long amount of time, you know that blisters can form and then turn to callus to protect the rawness on your hand. In just that way, over the years, I had laid down calluses of behavior that shielded me from my own rage and inability to fight my grandfather's abuse. Now in personal and professional relationships, I seemed to attract the most difficult persons, and somehow, I reasoned, it must be what I deserved. I had internalized a pattern from my grandfather, and over time, I changed my behavior to accommodate new emotional boundaries. I responded differently, not necessarily in a better way. I rebuilt my exterior self to match, so that I seemed impermeable and strong. But inside, I was paralyzed with fear. That is until someone hurt something helpless near me, like a horse in my training. Then I instinctively wanted to hurt the one doing the hurting.

Mary's threatening and aggressive handling of Renaissance stripped me raw until I could no longer stand by and do nothing. I finally asked her to leave my barn. I fumed that I'd ever had a part in her owning Renaissance. I feared now that I wouldn't be able to track the mare and somehow, as a result of all of it, felt less of a human. Humans should protect. Here I had just watched hurt grow and grow.

The day the trailer hauled Renaissance away, Mary sat stony-faced in the passenger seat of the hauler's truck. Her body language told me I'd wronged her, and everything was my fault.

I'd watched Mary's match with the horse decline past my ability to repair it; my relationship with my client and friend had disintegrated along with the horse's ability to understand the requests. And yet I sensed somehow they'd be back. Call it premonition. Hope, wounded though it was, still limped through my anger. I *wanted* our tracks to cross again.

Only a year later, the phone rang.

"I want to come back to your barn. I want to breed Renaissance to Eros."

My stallion was soon to be sold to a young rider who wanted a champion-quality jumper, and most likely would be gelded.

"I don't know—" I started to say.

"Come on, Shelley. We can work this out. Besides, good teachers are hard to find, and I want to take lessons again. I'm sorry. We can fix what went wrong."

I hesitated, knowing that how she treated Renaissance, and how we parted as trainer and student, didn't work for me. I couldn't repeat that relationship or its ending.

One of my friends and colleagues was Linda Kohanov, who created the Epona Center. There, she worked with people to heal emotional wounds and issues through a distinctive therapy program with horses. I'd worked with Linda and her clients for several years, and knew the successes she could have.

"I'll only take you back on one condition."

"What?" she said.

"If the experience starts to go south for either of us, we'll bring Linda in to work with us. That's not negotiable."

Mary agreed and we were off to another start.

The frustration the rider can feel in a training session when their horse isn't "getting it," or understanding what the rider wants, is often not so much about the horse but about the rider expressing their own familiar human impatience. It's as painful to watch as it is to experience. As a trainer, I can intellectualize a problem with a given horse and rider, but as important as evaluating the rider's and horse's skill together is the imperative to identify the signals passing between them. Is the communication clear? What is the individual story of each?

Over time and many horses and students, I've observed that physical corrections of horse behavior correct more than just the behavior; they alter the conversation. Sometimes for good, sometimes not. I've adjusted my training to accommodate this understanding of the effects of even the smallest tap of a whip. As others should have intervened for me as a child, I've learned to intervene for the horse. Learning to intervene with the humans, even my students, to reshape behavior, is still a new landscape for me.

It didn't take long after Mary's return to my barn for her way of dealing with her mare to sink back into a pattern of miscommunication. Our human timeline for success is way shorter and more urgent than the horse's own; a horse lives in the present, one event at a time. Mary had the signature middle-aged concerns about riding: Was she strong enough and brave enough to achieve what she wanted? Would learning how to ride this horse well happen quickly enough to leave her with enough years to enjoy and show the horse? Renaissance was as sensitive and intelligent as Mary.

The result? Rider insisted, horse resisted. Trainer insisted, rider resisted.

I wanted to tell her that working with resistance in a horse is like working a knot that will continue to tighten if you apply force in the wrong way at the wrong time. If force is your only option, you'd be better off stopping, or cutting the knot out of your thread before it becomes undoable. But the knots people create in their horses can get tight very, very quickly. And it can take a far better negotiator than me to clarify to the rider what's happening.

I was again watching a form of abuse, or perhaps more significantly, a neglect of honesty between rider and horse that I needed to stop. But given my history with Mary, I was apprehensive about tackling this volatile issue in her lessons. I'm just not all that good speaking human to my own kind.

Mary's frustration about her progress on a horse she knew was exceptionally talented burned slow and steady. Now she was angry with me because she was sure she was correctly riding the movements I asked her to perform, though I insisted she wasn't. What we were both forgetting was the effort it takes to be heard by each other at all. Couldn't I cut her some slack and see it her way, how hard this was for her? Dressage is a difficult and precise riding discipline. Couldn't she hear me? A slight aid from the rider can bring more from the horse than a heavy hand. A single word from a trainer can make the difference between hope and a sense of failure. But the rider and trainer must be patient and focus—listen, if you will.

Lesson by lesson, Mary rode with more aggression. And then one day, much like any other, the three of us reached crisis.

Show season had arrived, and Mary was finally ready to go.

For the first time since owning the mare and coming back to my barn, Mary was going to participate in the full show season. Excited for her progress, we prepared carefully and long. It was her second recognized—or rated—show of the season. I was overjoyed, and relieved to be here with her, to be a part of the growth she and Renaissance had achieved with such effort, and was proud of her for taking on the challenge.

The trouble slipped in as quietly as a feather landing on the surface of a pond.

Mary was tense in the warm-up arena, usual for anyone and especially for someone new to showing, but suddenly she came unglued. She was convinced that this had been the wrong thing to do.

"I can't do this," she said.

I did my best to calm her.

"You'll be fine—you've done all the right work to take the mare into this test and do really well." And I knew Renaissance could cover for Mary's shortcomings.

Mary's test was Training Level Test One. In dressage, this is an early test in a horse and rider's career, where your goal is to correctly master the basics that underlay all the harder movements as you go up the show levels. We heard the call for her test, and with more encouragement, I got Mary to enter the arena.

She executed her test without error, to receive a score of 58% on a scale of 100%. We had never talked about what she wanted to achieve as a percentage, and I thought this was very, very decent for her first effort.

"Hey!" I said, as she walked from the arena, "Pat your horse! I'm proud of you, you did great!"

I thought Mary was pleased. I surely was. To see a horse that I'd trained taking care of my student, and teaching her how to achieve in the show ring, was a great moment for me as a trainer.

But a storm loomed between horse and rider, and the thunder rumbled silently under Mary's skin. She wasn't satisfied. She wanted more. I had no idea how much I didn't understand human, and how much I hadn't heard Mary trying to tell me with her behavior.

She moved past, looking down at me from the saddle, and said nothing.

Mary knew that every movement she had seen her daughter, or me, perform on Renaissance, looked simple and effortless. But for her, replicating each aid was at best a chore and at worst, pure pain and failure. She considered her score not enough of a "win" and it infuriated her.

Mary wouldn't talk to me until the show was over. Anger has a way of starting on the cool side, then burning its way into speech and action.

On that morning of her lesson, the week after the show, a gust of air lifts a plastic bag from a corner in the tack room and lofts it into the barn aisle. Laramie, who was standing stock still as I wrapped her legs for work, stiffened to attention. At 17.3 hands and 1,800 pounds, my mare is an intense animal who is thoroughly at home in her body. In that comfort, she and I differ.

My long walking warm-up with Laramie lasted twenty-five minutes. We did many lateral movements: shoulder-in, haunches-in, half-pass. I used these suppling dressage movements to get her muscles to flow water-like into energy and impulsion. The walk time also just gave her a chance to wake fully into her job as dressage horse. I'd had her since she was three years old, so we knew each other well. Now that she was ten and grown up, her warm-up catalyzed her training session. Here I could gauge just how the ride would go; I could tell whether I could proceed with her to a new movement or only practice what we'd mastered the previous day. I competed with her at the FEI (Fédération Equestre Internationale), the upper levels of dressage. Laramie at times seemed to be doing her work on her own, and at those levels, you want to see that. It had taken long hard days, months, years to get to this place where we met each other each morning, hoof in hand.

For example, I had recently begun Laramie's work in place, or *passage*. *Passage* is a two-beat gait, or trot, in which the time one diagonal pair of legs is above ground is prolonged while the horse hesitates before traveling forward with the other diagonal pair of legs, like a trot in extreme slow motion. The *passage* gave me the sense that Laramie was floating between movements. Today, as we warmed up, I could feel Laramie celebrating the space she held on the planet, lightly dancing ever so slightly forward with each move of her legs. She would need the *passage* for next year's show season, but we would go slow learning the movement until it was body memory for her. Because of her size, it took more out of her physically to achieve the finesse and breath-long hesitation required between strides than it would have for a smaller horse of her skill.

Yes, I could rush this. Some trainers would. But the consciousness of each other as beings, and of our goal and need to move forward as partners, had a timing all its own.

As we worked, I listened to Laramie without an agenda. Most of the time, if I got in her way, she told me immediately with a swish of her tail or her ears rotating flat back to me. These not-so-subtle hints were warnings only for me, because she could end the lesson suddenly and forcefully whenever she wanted. All progress depended on this mostly silent language we cultivated.

I asked Laramie to extend into a regular trot, and circled her to the right, nearly finished with our ride. After a little more stretching she'd be free of me and this workout.

Mary's car had pulled up while I worked Laramie. She gave me a perfunctory wave, then headed into the darkness of the barn to saddle Renaissance.

I thought about how Mary and I worked well together as long as she was willing to work on her own personal issues out of the saddle, and keep them off her horse's back. Horses intuit everything through their backs, sides, mouths. Our tension probably feels like muttering to them. Anger or frustration is like a scream. The tension between us at the show was something I worried I'd see in her saddle today.

The cool December wind coaxed up dust devils to dance in tiny mad whorls down the center line. Not as warm as yesterday, the sky was a milky shade of blue, and I sensed a weather shift. My body responded before my mind processed the feeling: Mary and I were picking up the mood of the show from the previous weekend. I thought I knew what her personal issues would be today, but even so I'd guessed wrong. I couldn't even imagine the truth.

Laramie and I passed the opening into the arena as Mary and Renaissance entered. She wore sunglasses, so I couldn't tell by her eyes if her mood was good. I only said hello, respecting her quietness. I realized watching Renaissance walk how much I really cared about this mare. I had owned Renaissance or had her in my training since she was two, so I knew her well. Now she was seventeen and I had sold her to Mary, and our own personal struggles and miscommunications made training either of them harder. I was angry at Mary and fearful for the horse. I worried that I'd lose all contact with the mare if Mary left with her again, and worse, I felt less human for failing Mary.

At least for now, both of them were back in my barn. The arena offered a canvas on which to paint another lesson in Horse Meets Human. Or in my case, Human Meets Human on Horseback.

As her lessons did more and more often, this one took the predictable and ugly turn early.

Before she mounted up, Mary dug into her pocket for something. Her hand brought an image to my mind, of me carrying the events of my life in my pockets. Some days I needed extra pockets to hold all the questions I'd worn smooth as I worried them, trying to figure out how I got to this place, and how to stay in one piece. My hand drifted to my own hip as I walked Laramie on a loose rein. I valued the questions as much, maybe more, than the answers. Questions had edges and potential. If I handled them enough, I could reshape them into smoother answers. Mary was a question nestled in my pocket, as was Renaissance's future. By finding the answers that could fit them, I might heal something in me.

Every day, every ride, Renaissance had her own story to tell. I began Mary's lesson, working from atop Laramie, and already I sensed an electric beginning.

I asked Mary to trot and she did, but the mare's back quickly hollowed and dropped away from her seat, and her head came high. Mary responded by bracing her own frame and fussing with Renaissance's mouth. Her fingers started nervously, pulsing Morse code to the mare's tongue and lips, but her hands quickly escalated to war on the reins. She bumped the mare squarely in the mouth, over and over. Worse, when Renaissance's head lifted, Mary gave up and made her walk, then started over. I watched but said nothing, as the emotion changed into frustration in the horse and anger in her rider.

When a rider corrects a horse's behavior physically, she corrects more than the behavior. She alters the language between herself and the animal. Sometimes the change is good, but not always. A perfect riding aid or instruction applies just enough adjustment, just in time. I can't let even the smallest misapplication of correction slide. As others should have intervened for me as a child, in my work I've learned to intervene for the horse—they are trusting beings on the whole. Learning to intervene with the humans who are my students, to reshape their behavior just as carefully and look out for them, has always been the harder task for me as trainer.

"You can't keep that up," I said as Mary walked yet again. "You're *rewarding* her for putting her head up by walking her."

Mary didn't respond. The fussing continued.

My students often want success immediately. It's human—we get tired of waiting and working for results that are subtle, and our patience frays and then snaps. The horse, on the other hand, doesn't have a timeline, and always lives in the present moment, one event at a time. I could see Mary clearly wanted success right now, not by next show season, and not even at the next lesson. Now. I knew it; she knew it. If I couldn't communicate the impossibility here, we'd fail again.

"Mary!"

Rider insisted, horse resisted. Horse insisted, rider resisted.

"If you keep rewarding her for putting her head up by walking," I said, "pretty soon she'll only have her head up because it means she *gets* to walk."

Mary leaped off the mare to the ground, pulling her head around with the reins. In one swing, she slashed Renaissance across the chest with her whip, as hard as I'd ever seen a rider strike a horse.

Laramie and I stopped. I couldn't breathe. That slash was meant as much for me, across my chest or ribs, as for Renaissance. *If I told, my grandfather had said, I'd die.* But not speaking was killing me. For a second time, I would have to ask Mary to leave my barn. But this time only the pattern of bad behavior, not me, would die. I would end it. Renaissance couldn't speak human. Only I could tell for her.

I whispered to Mary, and then repeated myself louder.

"We promised each other to go to Linda if things got bad again. Do you remember?"

My voice echoed the hurt and loneliness of having been betrayed. I'd let her back in my space but she did nothing to change her behavior.

I slid from Laramie's back and walked her to the barn, finding my cell phone on the wire chair just inside the door. I knew it wasn't my call to make, and as I looked back to the arena to reconsider, I saw Mary at her car, barely holding the mare's reins in one hand, and talking into her cell phone with her head tucked deep to her chest. I could tell she was leaving a message because she talked without pause for a response. Mary's shoulders slumped, and the barrel of Renaissance's chest shuddered in and out as the mare struggled to regain her breath.

I set my cell phone back on the chair, and led Laramie, still hot, out to the mounting block again. Riding felt better than standing; talking, or trying to, seemed far better than fuming. Taking my example, Mary mounted too.

The only trust between us now was for the horses we rode. The shifting grind of sand under the horses' hooves rubbed sound into the air. The horses stepped behind each other, down the long side of the arena, around a corner, and up the other side. Mary trotted to come next to me.

She pulled the sunglasses off her face and talked to me in a desperate rush.

"I didn't mean it, Shelley. You have to know Renaissance is the only being next to Emma that I love at all. If my relationship with this horse stops working, I don't have much left."

The torrent started, the storm began, and rage flooded out. Mary talked and talked. She offered me excruciatingly hard details about her anger and the abuse in her own life, how she seemed to hurt what she loved. This was a behavior so ingrained in her that now she can't even remember how she got this way. When she is in fear of her own safety, caused by the mare's head-tossing and increasingly angry behavior, she only knows to lash out first. It's the only way she knows to protect herself. Or even to stay loved. Hurt first, so you're in control. Hitting her horse was the last thing she meant to do. She also told me her fury at me was real, and she couldn't get rid of it. I wondered if it meant I mattered to her more than she knew.

"Why can't you help me, Shelley, why can't I *make* her respond? Why can't you help me *make* her? I don't want to hurt her, but she takes it from me. I can't hit you, but I sure want to. I love this horse and I hate what I do. I'm so trapped. All I can do is hit her because she'll take it. I want her to love me back by showing me she'll do what I ask."

From the back of the small mare, Mary looked up at me on Laramie.

"So what's your story?" she asked me, spent and honest in her questioning. "Because I know you're shocked and angry at me. I can tell. What are you thinking?"

Tears can't water the desert—they evaporate as quickly as they fall. But between us, this water was enough to moisten the hardpan of our anger. Both of us cried.

If I told her my own past, I risked something different. I might form a new pattern. Or I might give away any power I had to keep myself safe. I spoke.

"I have so much pain, Mary, that only the horse is safe for me. Only the horse. So I'm desperate and fierce when you hurt her. You're hurting my safety."

Waiting for her to respond, I thought that I wasn't so different from her. We were a sisterhood of mares and women, fighting off anger and hurt when it happened to us, for reasons that had left language behind. We had to talk to each other and let the anger out, to transform the pain to one clear pool of water that we could share and drink from to keep us alive.

So we rode and talked, as hard as it was, until both of us began to soften. I shared small bits of my past, and she did too, the words quenching some fire between us. Without having said a thing about the lesson, I offered something new to this woman, whom I realized I cared about as both student and friend. She became pliant, less resistant. This lesson opened two parched hearts.

I am always relearning human, a sharp and difficult language. But it has to work because it is all we have to salve each other's hurt. The stakes are very high. A heart made desert through fear, isolation, and abuse, risks dying thirsty.

One word at a time, one story at a time between us, Mary and I shed pain like old skin. Both horses, sensing the release, exhaled, and walked on.

7
Counter Change

Fear can suffocate a horse-and-rider relationship, or a relationship between two humans, slowly and efficiently. Like smoke, it settles over and permeates the rider's self-confidence, and snuffs the animal's ability to interpret other signals because he's too preoccupied worrying about the "thing out there." Who or what starts the fear response is irrelevant compared to its effect.

By contrast, fear's simple opposite—trust—is even more subtle in working a change in horse and rider. One tiny moment of things going well builds on another, and over time, the rider and horse accumulate enough things that went well to be able to rely on each other's composure. "I'll be strong for you, and vice versa," sort of.

Fear and trust differ in the direction each takes. Fear can't seem to move in a straight line; it wavers, steps side to side, a little forward, then back, until it gathers enough rocking, unbalanced momentum to fall straight into terror. Trust moves forward like a current in a clear creek, steady and sure. It washes into and fills the spaces between the rider's worry and the horse's anticipation, until both, filled and satisfied, can risk looking behind them.

So what do horses fear? Other creatures that could eat them. Bright lights, unexpected sounds or movement. If they get hurt, something about the incident or the recovery can stay in memory and shade all the rest of their behavior. What do humans fear? Loss of control, pain. Unexpected events that can devastate them personally. Not so different from a horse in some respects. A horse can react fearfully to being handled by too many humans. A person can fear being handled at all. A horse can imprint on a person and react very badly to that person's going away or to its sale to another person. A person can choose a partner who leaves, and as a result, fear ever having to make a choice again. A horse never has the choice, just the ability to react.

Trust can only build a little at a time, so what matters in the end is what direction you want to move—side to side or forward.

Sara and Meadow crossed my path because of a mutual friend in Seattle. Leah, who had taken lessons with me in Tucson, asked if I would be willing to come up and give weekend clinics at her place on the west side of Puget Sound, every two to three months, summer through fall. This is when Tucson's show season slows anyway and it's melting hot in the desert.

No matter the weather, horse people have a rough time getting away, let alone taking vacations, without some worry. As a competitive show rider with a training clientele in Tucson, a dog who has never flown but I'm sure would hate it, and all kinds of reasons to keep myself in one spot, I worry more than most about leaving. But my friend was persuasive, offering me the chance to return to the Northwest after twenty years in the Southwest with few breaks. The idea of an early vacation, even a working one, sounded fine. I rationalized it as the chance to try out my skills with new riders, like Sara, and promised myself I would just call home every day to make sure my own horses were all right.

In the first clinic, Leah arranged for five riders to school over three days of lessons with me; they all were riding with me solely on Leah's recommendation. I was nervous. It was June of 2003, and I arrived a day earlier than I needed because I wanted time to settle into my own skin.

As I left the airport, I savored something I realized I'd missed—green. Seattle glowed emerald and olive. The air, washed by recent rains of smog and dust, smelled salty and fresh. I'd arranged to stay at a hotel in the Pike Place Market neighborhood, close to downtown Seattle. I wanted time to think about things over the taste of fresh raspberries and other fruit too delicate and water-thirsty to grow well in Tucson.

I knew from our schedule that the next day I needed ride a ferry from Seattle across Puget Sound and arrive in time for Leah to pick me up for the lessons that would start by noon. So I tried to fill these twenty-four hours with the taste of just-caught seafood, walks past the produce vendors' high stalls, and poking over crafts of all kinds. I thought about being here as a kid, and how much I remembered and now missed—all triggered by scents and the sky stretching out over water. From my room, a view of steely Puget Sound and the barely snow-laced Olympic mountains far in the distance soothed the red desert heat from my thoughts. I did wonder about the riders I'd meet, but it almost didn't matter. This was the vacation. Not a horse in sight.

At night, settling in, I reread the e-mail Leah sent me about the riders.

"Lucy competes in three-day eventing and has a new draft-mixed-with-Warmblood gelding named Guinness; he's black and big boned, purchased in British Columbia... Nikki has ridden a long time, has a Canadian Warmblood, and needs some confidence-building with her mare... Neva, a Goth teenager, has a rose gray, tiny Oldenburg mare, Risky. She's riding because Nikki is her riding teacher, and her mother is Nikki's friend, and both think Neva needs to be around women who don't wear black... You know that I have my chestnut gelding, Orias... And Sara will ride Meadow, a gray Arabian mare she's care-leasing. That'll be a tough one."

I had no doubt it would be interesting.

One of the principles that riders who study dressage learn early is the concept of "forward," or how to keep the horse's energy moving from his hind end through and over his back, into your hands and finally, into the track ahead. Without forward, you have nothing. Certainly you can't insist that the animal tighten its movement and mold that building energy into the dance of cooperation that is dressage.

If I were to tack up Laramie, have you mount up in my dressage saddle, and ask you to look down from her back, you would see the front of your saddle and Laramie's neck from above. You would notice how your reins attach to a bit, how stirrup leathers hold the irons on which you rest your feet, and how balancing yourself, torso over legs, makes you *almost* ready to ask her to move. If I trustingly handed you a dressage whip, and gave you spurs to extend the reach of your leg (remember, Laramie is my girl, and I'm extremely careful with her), you'd possess the simple tools to use with your body to ask for forward. But nothing really can move Laramie forward but your desire. You need to be ready to request the energy, and prepared for it coming through your body and into your hands, whatever that will feel like. You also need to be prepared for her to lose it if your mind wanders and you happen to stop wanting forward with every part of yourself.

Forward movement in walk, trot, and canter covers ground. You're not dawdling on a rental stable's horse who knows to take it easy because it's going to be a long day. On a big fresh horse, as Laramie is, it can seem fast. But on any horse it feels like more than a thousand pounds of muscle doing what it does best—preparing to run like hell from whatever is out there. Most of us, on a strange horse, wouldn't notice fear touching the small of our backs as we lose our focus. It's easy to swallow your heart for a second too long and think about the cost—you could fall, the horse could shy. In that second, fear settles closer behind you in the saddle. You might not notice it; but your horse feels its vaporous weight instantly.

From Laramie's perspective, she doesn't know you, but she's let you get up on her back because she trusts *me*. That's as far as I can help, however, because now you're in charge. She can see your legs, sense your seat bones shifting, taste the vibration your hands cause on her bit, and smell the thought you're having about the "thing out there." In each ride, you need to build trust with her moment by moment, and as you wait, you're losing ground.

But let's imagine you're strong, and you get past this small worry about what her movement will feel like, and you ask her to walk on. I'm the bossy trainer, and I tell you to come off the rail that bounds the arena and instead of going straight, to walk the mare in a circle around me while I watch. You have to keep her moving forward with energy. Being a horse, and sensing your reluctance to have something happen, Laramie offers resistance to a circle because she knows straight is less work—and a horse's instinct is to save energy to run from something truly frightening. This was your idea to up the demand, after all.

I'm no help because I'm not in the saddle. You get frustrated and ask with more intent, maybe pulling the reins to turn. But you're concentrating on turning, and you forget about forward; you're asking for only a fraction of what you need. Worse, you only *think* you're asking and what you're really saying in your head to the horse sounds like, "Turn, damn it."

In my experience, the horse heard this through your body and hands before it left your mind. This kind of anxiety in the rider, over several more small movements, can fan the "thing out there" into something tangible to fear (horses easily engage with fear without your asking them to). You're well on your way to the horse spooking at invisible terrors because that fear has to come out somewhere. Horses also love a good adrenaline rush.

But is Laramie really ignoring you? No. She responds by raising her head, hollowing her back, and making her reluctant circle in sharp angles instead of curves. Her trust—in you, your aids, and your hands—weakens, surely and relentlessly. This ride deteriorates into a stalemate of wills.

I ask you to bring Laramie back to me, and I let you hop off. I just didn't want you to think this was going to be easy.

Leah picked me up at the ferry, and I walked off to meet her, knowing that I had five lessons to teach. I am very shy by nature and a little gruff when I'm in a new situation, but in a riding arena I am at peace because I have spent most of my life there. I would be nervous only until my feet touched arena footing.

We got to her place on time, but because the first rider was still tacking up, I took the time to put my luggage away before returning outside so that I met the first rider only after she was up and warming her horse. In other words, I started late. In Tucson, I'm never late. All of my students will find this hard to believe: I never ran on time in Seattle. I was always twenty to thirty minutes behind the schedule Leah arranged. I think horse people are known for their tardiness, and usually, I won't be a part of that. Only in Seattle, it felt like I was fitting into the mold starting late, and every lesson ran over into the next one. It felt good, this freedom to wait for the natural start and end of things. This clinic is where I started to see a different way to be with my students.

We worked hard from early to late afternoon. I liked these riders. The women listened thoughtfully and applied my advice, both to different challenging behavioral issues in their respective horses, and seat position or hand issues in themselves. The interactions felt truthful and genuine. Each finished rider returned to sit and watch the next, and as the time wore on, a sense of being in the right place settled over me. By 4:00 p.m., we'd reached the last lesson of the day.

"We have a problem for you, if you're up for it," Leah said to me.

I watched as a petite and blonde young woman led a small gray Arabian mare into the arena.

"Meadow's a handful. She got kicked in the stifle as a two-year-old, and cantering is something she doesn't do easily. She's off balance. It makes for an interesting ride—sort of a run-like-hell thing. Lots of inconsistent riders worked her before Sara. Her owner has a lot of horses to take care of."

"So is that the problem?" I said.

"Not exactly. There's something more to this, and we can't figure it out. She's running when she canters, and she doesn't have a left lead. If she does nail it, she's kind of insane about it. Might be a soundness issue, might be Arabness." Leah smiled. The Arab breed is known for its intelligence and wiliness. Be careful what you teach them; they remember everything.

Sara, mounted now, seemed calm, and the softness in the mare's eyes confirmed she was also at ease. The other riders pitched in what they knew about Sara; she was somewhere in her thirties, was "care-leasing" Meadow—providing grooming care in exchange for riding privileges. Sara had adored the mare from the time the filly was two years old. Meadow's owners bred Arabians, and Meadow was their first foal. They had accumulated too many for one person to ride, and both husband and wife had full-time jobs off the property. Over the years, through an old gentleman who lived with the owners and knew of and spoke well for Sara, she was engaged to exercise the other horses for them. She'd had an aging Arab gelding who she'd brought to board there, but in time she'd had to find a retirement place for him. She now worked Meadow, and really hoped to own the mare somehow, Leah told me, waiting for the owners to offer her the chance to buy her. Or, in the best of all worlds, Sara hoped to exchange her care for ownership. She'd invested in riding lessons on Meadow, daily work in basic dressage, and had built trust with the horse. Watching the interactions between this horse and rider, I could tell that there was an unusually strong bond between them, but I couldn't see just how deep it was, or what made it. Sometimes strength isn't strong at all; it's just a worn place in a pattern we find comfort in.

A canter is a three-beat gait, and to most nonriders it looks like a gallop. The canter's "lead" is determined by which front leg leads at the end of a full stride. If the right hind strikes off first, then the diagonal pair of left hind and right front legs strike together, finishing in the left front—a left lead. Just before leaving Tucson, I had worked with another gray horse who had a problem cantering on a left lead. I had no magic cure for her, just more patience and willingness to repeat the aids correctly than her owner did. That mare, also Arabian, caught on.

Sara hadn't said more than hello yet, and since I am a bit nervous whenever I have to approach a new person, I decided to break the quiet first and walked into the arena to be closer to her.

"So what's going on?" I said, watching Sara's body language. She wasted no time to pull up next to me. She straightened her helmet and looked off in the distance as she started talking. Her voice remained calm and matter of fact, but a tight cord in her neck gave away her tension.

"Well, I ride her all the time. But no matter what I do, the thing of it is, I can't get her to take a left lead," she said. "She just keeps trotting faster and faster and breaks into a right lead. I've tried everything."

"Everything?" I said with a smile.

"Everything. She was kicked a long time ago, and I can't tell if she's weak on that side, or if I'm cueing her wrong. It's frustrating. I've tried everything."

"Everything usually does it. But walk her in a circle on a loose rein for me."

I saw no issues right away. The lovely gray head and neck swung with each stride, and Sara didn't show resistance either.

"Trot for me, but still keep her on a loose rein. Don't worry if she responds with speed to the loose rein. I just want her to go forward."

She let her mare relax into the gait, completing many circles.

"Now pick up your reins a bit and ask her to really move forward."

She may have been a small mare, but Meadow had big gaits. It seemed the canter would just *have* to be there, effortlessly, when I asked Sara for the transition.

The ride changed. The mare got frantic. Sara tried again, and again, from that bold trot asking for canter, and always Meadow struck the right lead instead of left on the circle. Her out-of-balance ride and tense jaw showed something was really wrong.

"Ohhhh-kay..." I said, drawing the word out and the tone down to relax the mare and rider. "Just...walk..." Both breathed heavily.

"May I try?" I asked.

"Sure," Sara said, swinging off and down with a quickness that said, "I've had it." I walked Meadow to the mounting block and got up. After a few trot circles, I gave her the aid to strike off on a left lead. It didn't work, but I'm patient with horses. I let everything about what I'd seen drain away from me. I breathed deeply, moved forward, not holding any history of what I'd seen in the saddle, and tried again. This time, she picked up a left lead, although I could sense through my seat and hands how unstable Meadow felt about her movement on that side. She cantered without balance, shaking her head, worried. I brought her back to a trot, then a walk, and then back to a left lead. I repeated this several times, and finally asked Sara to get back up.

"You need to trust her," I said. "It's not about you. She doesn't have a lot of experience doing this well, and it's foreign to her." I suspected this way of being with a horse was foreign to Sara as well, asking and waiting a breath, and asking again.

Sara trotted Meadow once more, and I could tell she trusted me to get her through this. But that didn't make it a sure thing with Meadow. I'd performed no magic in the saddle, just changed the conversation. Sara was trying to listen to this horse she loved, but clearly something else frustrated her.

"She's worried," I repeated to Sara. "It's not really misbehavior."

Sara's jaw set as she asked the mare to canter again. Meadow tore through the first circle unbalanced and on the wrong lead.

"Meadow doesn't get that this doesn't have to feel bad, Sara. Just relax. Just keep circling and stay with her. It has to come from you."

"It's not working," she said.

"Keep going forward. It doesn't matter if she gets it yet. Keep focused and don't get mad. She's not trying to evade you. She just doesn't trust this thing we're trying to do. And right now, she doesn't know if she should trust either one of us. *You* have to trust first."

Sweat streaked Sara's face. The evening was warm, and she struggled for the correct lead. I couldn't tell if she could sense the mare's worry through her hands as I could, but circle after circle at the trot showed her easing a little of her grip, and by teaspoons her own fear of something bad happening started to evaporate into the air. The mare's neck muscles lengthened as she stretched to the bit.

"There. Now let her go, stay loose," I said. "You have to be ready when she is."

I couldn't count the circles she made, but one after another they came and blurred the separateness of horse and rider into a single form in this gold green evening time and place. She asked gently, her body and hands now expectant of this ease they'd found.

Without fanfare, Meadow transitioned to a left lead canter, still fast but moving forward with grace that showed through a fluid neck and back. She and Sara were lovely together.

"Perfect," I said, "Let her walk."

The relief felt like a cool breeze, though none blew, as Sara brought her to a walk, and then stopped. What I'd taken for sweat on her cheeks had changed to the sweeter rain of light tears. As my own tears met Sara's, Meadow's gaze grew soft and liquid, and she blew out a deep breath. I let my soul sigh out. Change like this is powerful, and deserves much respect with silence.

As a trainer, I get horses who hide a lot of themselves from me. They don't choose to, but it's how they've learned to feel safe. Just keep going, no matter what. Few experience a mental break where they can no longer work, but it does happen. I can feel something riding with me, but they can't tell me what "it" is. When I hide what hurts or vanish from myself in moments of extreme stress, it's the same feeling of going numb. I can't breathe or act; I can only wait in that place. To stay present and go forward can hurt like hell. Surely the horses suffer as much. But the riders do too. Sara let go of something out there. Nothing else would have made that possible.

What I tried to show Sara was how not to be afraid of the movement that was happening, to feel herself and the mare, and sense how unconditionally, and hard, Meadow was trying to please her. She responded to what I can only believe was a change in her rider: Sara allowed the mare space to be frightened in, but never left her there alone. She stayed and offered back trust. She didn't punish her for failing. So the mare—sensing Sara listening—absorbed the trust and found the correct lead.

By this time the women sitting on the grass by the arena were standing amazed. Overcoming something old and hardened in myself that has to be reminded, often, of this simple trust lesson, I marveled at how it could appear fresh to me again and again.

I traveled up to Washington for a second and a third clinic, and in each one the improvement in both rider and horse exceeded what I'd hoped to see. In the second clinic, to see how far the trust between

Meadow and Sara had really come, I suggested that Sara try a device created by Linda Tellington-Jones that made it possible for someone to ride bridle-free. The simple device of a rawhide loop or "necklace," which goes over the horse's head and rests lightly around the neck, allows you to focus only on your balance and take the weight off your hands. Ultimately you can ride without even a bridle if you choose, steering, stopping, all without effort. You ride from your seat, legs, and heart.

Sara laughed and patted Meadow at the end of a lesson, and thinking about the rawhide loop, said she wasn't sure it was time just yet.

At the third clinic, I brought the loop to her. Meadow's owners had come over to watch their mare work with Sara.

"You ready?" I asked her.

"Sure," Sara said. "No problem."

I slipped the rawhide loop over Meadows head, and it settled around the base of her neck. I showed Sara how to use it as if it were a solid rein, pulling back lightly to slow Meadow, tugging on one side or the other to turn, and how to slide it higher on the neck if more control was needed. With the bridle still on Meadow, but with her reins tied to hang loosely from her neck, Sara walked off with her hands free, not holding the loop. At the trot, she started her circle, and within a few rounds, she asked for a left-lead canter. I didn't need to say anything, nor could I have added much to help this pair do any better. Sara and Meadow melded into one form.

The owners were delighted.

"Good girl, Meadow" they called, "What a good girl." The owners applauded the mare round after round. I didn't know if they understood what had happened in this partnership. It wasn't all Meadow.

Sara's smile tightened, but she stayed up and stroked the mare's neck as she cooled her out.

I also didn't understand why Sara was risking the moon here with a horse she didn't own. Her reasons might have been these: She had decided that whatever the outcome of owning this horse, all of the trust gained here and now was worth it. Or, she was holding on to the dream of owning Meadow, in which case this trust display had to demonstrate to the owners how worthy she'd become of taking on their first foal permanently. As I watched her slide off, I thought of another possibility: She always knew how unavailable this creature was to her, but chose her in an unconscious self-defeating way anyhow. She might not want to lose the chance to have her, but if she did, she could be angry at the owners instead of at herself for choosing something she couldn't really ever have in the first place.

I know about sabotaging relationships of any sort. When I do it, I'm falling back into a pattern of not remembering that in that moment, I'm worth more than what I'm choosing for myself. I also *want* the dangerous thing, and am not satisfied by the nagging advice I hear from myself, gleaned from so many lessons where I knew, but still chose what wasn't right, and then got hurt. I know the extremes I've paid for risking so much. As her teacher and friend, I wanted a different outcome for Sara.

I knew how far she'd come in her riding and that the horse she chose to work with could mean a lot for where her skill might grow. Her limited resources for lessons and care meant she couldn't have two horses to ride, Meadow—if the owner wouldn't sell her or give her to Sara—or any different horse. After the bridleless ride, I decided to ask her the hard question.

"Do you really think they'll let you have Meadow?"

"They have to see how good we are together."

"With everything that happened today, would you be willing to spend more of your own time and money if Meadow won't ever be yours?"

"I can't afford another horse. They know that. They have too many now, and can't ride them all. I'm the one who puts in the time on her."

Sara didn't want to go down that road. Her belief in the gift Meadow gave her was proof that anything was possible. I know from a horse owner's point of view that even if you don't ride that horse all the time, it's still your horse. Meadow's owners had no real reason to sell her. They'd bred her, and had the property to keep her. Sara wasn't blind to these facts. So I thought about all the people I've encountered, including me, who want to love something or someone unconditionally, despite the cost. Wanting unconditional affection, we find it sometimes only in the creatures who bring us no conditions. Humans by nature are conditional.

"You need to talk to them, Sara. Do you want me to ask? I do know of another horse that would also be good for you."

"Ask," Sara said. But I think she just saw my offer as the intervention that would help her gain Meadow. She didn't think the owners would want her to give up Meadow.

I had a friend in a medical residency program in Kentucky who'd called me on my cell phone that morning. She was desperate. The horse she'd bought to finally be her ultimate dressage horse had just finished having surgery for lameness, and needed time and attention she just didn't have as a young doctor. I mentioned the horse to Sara.

"He could be yours for the price of shipping. He needs care, but Cosmic is a really great guy. He's a dressage horse, big gray. You'd really like him."

She looked at me firmly, a small smile forming that said no without saying "no."

"I want to see what they say about Meadow. I can walk away if I have to."

Shortly after the clinic, I wrote a note to Meadow's owners and mailed it from Tucson. I wanted them to have the time to think about my question, without the immediacy that e-mail or a phone call can impose. I let them know I had a horse in mind for Sara, but that she was sure that Meadow would be hers one day, and did they know that? The owners responded a few days later: Having bred and raised Meadow, they told me clearly that they intended to keep her. Sara was welcome to ride her as long as she liked, but they had no desire to sell her.

After I shared the news with Sara, she got angry and stopped riding Meadow. The owners were puzzled, but took Meadow back into their herd with ease and never looked back. Not all horse or love stories end happily. Most just end. The horse is sold, the lover leaves, the friend breaks a promise we are sure they made and we are crushed.

Sara knew Meadow was unavailable. But Sara feared trusting her instinct and moving forward. I think the truth about love is that it always has a price, even if it involves a horse. I have met a lot of women in the training I do with horses who invest heavily in unconditional love for their animal. The price is always high, even if it's just the cost of keeping the horse. No matter how much you love them, they're horses. Sometimes, you lose the animal because they colic, or you sell the horse because you've divorced and can't afford to keep it, or you physically move and can't take the horse with you. In a worst case, what or who you love can simply never be yours.

Does this mean you should or do stop loving what you can't have? Of course not. When we insist in our belief for a different ending we can find a lesson—if you disregard wisdom, and take the high road of the heart, no matter the outcome, you learn to trust and navigate from your heart. We can and will be fearful of any loss. But taking the reins—or letting go in Sara's case—and trusting what you feel can let your heart teach you almost anything, even to fly on the back of your white, unavailable mare in the only moments she will ever be yours. The time you have with anything or anyone you love is counted like this—moment by moment, heartbeat after heartbeat.

My Washington friend offered to board the new horse, Cosmic, if Sara wanted to take him, and to take him on herself if Sara and he didn't work out together. So Sara is trying out this new horse, loving again unconditionally. He's gray, like Meadow, but he's enormous where Meadow was petite. He may remain sound, maybe not. Anything can happen with a horse.

But sometimes I wonder if in Sara's dreams, her heart plays her a story with images of its own hope and making—and whether it shows her riding big Cosmic or petite Meadow, bridleless on the left-lead canter. I might bet on Meadow. Because in dream space where time pauses still and quiet, you can have what you can't in daylight. There, her heart can take its time to wake her back to her work with Cosmic—until she perfects the ride she wants on the mare and puts her away in a barn built to hold love unconditionally.

8
Cosmic

Some days when I am dealing with people, I walk right up to the edge of a canyon. Stretched across that sheer-walled space between me and the other person swings what feels to me like a frail rope bridge over a breath-snatching drop. I hesitate to cross. On my side, I know comfort in my solitude; on the other side, I sense intimacy and its friend, risk. If I get to the other side, I can have both, just maybe, in the human who waits ahead. On some days, I step on and start to walk. On others, a wind comes up—like a cry from the other person asking me to let go, be vulnerable, give up my time and energy to them, *be with them*—and I begin to sway dangerously on my bridge. So I retreat. I'm reluctant to trust anyone to consistently give me what I need, and I don't believe easily that I can give them what they want from me. It's very hard to trust, let alone love.

Without hesitation, however, I give animals the grace to enter and be with me, just as they are. No surprise, then, that I've found it easier to interact with animals than humans. When I hurt, I seek the company of Laramie or my dog Boboli long before I think to wonder where my partner is. My animals regard me with openness and delight that I'm simply present in their day. They don't need to know details; I don't need to tell them how hard it is to find my footing with another person. Their plain agenda is love, comfort, and maybe dinner. They give me their attention and trust without question.

Animals are affectionate without conditions. I can anticipate a positive response when I run my hand over my horse's shoulder. My dog looks for me and expects to be petted, but if I don't, he doesn't turn away. He waits until I'm ready for him, and he is there when it happens. I can't expect a human to be that patient, and I can't predict, for a partner or friend or client, that I'll be able to wait patiently either. By habit, if I don't watch myself, I retreat in advance, and wait for them to enter. Sometimes someone bravely comes in. More often, I've made a gulf wide enough for them to worry about crossing, leaving me to choose whether to get on that bridge over my canyon.

At the end of my day, I am the only one who can convince myself that humans can be honorable. Because of what happened to me, I retreat. I respond similarly to the way any animal does to mistreatment. But animals—and this is remarkable—put aside the hurt, and try again with a human who offers them consistent steady kindness. So how do I do that?

I've tried to explain this to a friend time and again, and she always says, "But you must be saying something more. Maybe you're using the animals as a way to avoid the human interactions."

One day, at her home near Seattle, we were preparing to sit down to a feast of fresh Dungeness crab. If you've never had these sweet beauties from the Northwest on your plate, you're missing something fine. I bought them on my way from the airport, stopping in Seattle's Pike Place Market. I am from Tucson, so when the fisherman asked me if I wanted them cracked and cleaned, I had no idea and I said "no." At the house, my friend didn't remember the best way into the orange shells. Kenny, her husband, stood at the kitchen counter with us. After some joking with me that I "didn't have a clue as an Arizonan" about crab, he confessed that as a northern Idaho boy he wasn't sure he knew either.

"Honey..." my friend said tentatively, "would you call the market and ask them how we do it?"

His red bearded jaw set like iron.

"No, you call."

"Why?"

"You can call."

"Why won't you?"

"Because I don't want to." It was the end of the work day; he looked tired. I believed him that he didn't want to talk to anyone but us. I knew the feeling well. But there was something else at play here.

"Fine, I'll do it myself," she said.

A strained moment of quiet fell on our little feast. I said something to my friends to lighten the mood, and though he certainly didn't call, Kenny returned to his pleasant and amiable self. Needless to say it's not rocket science to open a crab's shell, and we easily figured it out.

But the next day, I offered this exchange in conversation to my friend as a classic example of my point. She wanted a simple thing from Kenny, and if she couldn't have that, she expected some small kind response at least, something that probably meant to her, "I love you, I know this is important to you." Her husband, tired and probably just wishing he could put his feet up somewhere, wanted to be taken care of too, and "care" to him looked like not having to make any decisions about dinner or call anyone about crab since his job, like his wife's, is full of encounters and phone calls.

"You wanted just that small kindness," I told her over coffee under a clear Northwest morning sky. "Can you see why it takes extra thought for me to let a human have the benefit of the doubt? I try, but it always gets tangled. My dog loves me unconditionally and would do anything for me if he could. It's a lot harder to ask for even part of that from a person."

She smiled at me with that "Whatever you say, Shelley" look that meant she still felt animals were just easier for me to handle.

Animals don't speak the human language; we trust each other if our bodies and thoughts say we can. I just don't get the same read off people.

One Tucson morning, early enough for the sun to have barely warmed the tile floor in our bedroom, I woke to the pressure of Boboli's curled back pushing into the spoon of my legs. I had one arm stretched the length from under my pillow to my partner's pillow, and I could feel the weight of her head on it, and the surrounding coolness where my fingers left the case and touched their surface. The air so quiet and calm, all I wanted was to pull her closer to me, but instead, in one thought, I knew if I touched her and got no response, it would wreck the moment. With my other arm draped over the sheet on my hip, I reached back and idly ran my fingers over Boboli's sleek torso, then rolled back to get up and going.

I've encountered so many animals in my work, abused and whole, who just want to be near me. Around them, I don't feel abandoned or broken. I don't fear "intimacy" with them—and I use that term differently here from how I mean it with a person. But because animals and humans can only interact through touch, smell, and sound of voice, everything about the relationship is "intimate," skin on skin. It's not about power, either, which as an incest survivor I fear most—losing myself to another, losing control over myself during sex or under a human's touch or even in a verbal encounter, because that's what my grandfather took from me. If I give in to intimacy, I have to *know* my human partner won't fail me. That's trust. Animals take me as I am. Nothing needs healing between us. For that, I love them and delight in the medicine they are for me. But I know the lesson they offer me is that I have to do this with humans, too, to be ready for the opportunity, and trust it when it comes.

When I am immersed in a passion, like my riding or my pen-and-ink drawings, I give myself to it utterly. I correct small mistakes with smaller aids, savoring infinite adjustments of seat or leg from the saddle, or straightness of line on the page. I don't question that the perfecting of these movements takes time and patience. As I ride a balanced dressage horse, I am one with that animal's spirit and heart. I am in love with the sensation of being "with" the animal. I don't need to talk about how it feels or what I expect in the future.

Human encounters are the last frontier of love for this survivor.

Maybe a human can begin to heal with a simple loving response from an animal, from the connection and the exchange of tenderness, the gaze from a soft eye. The light brush of my hand on the neck of a horse or the fur of a dog gives me peace. My time stills into the moment. My animals live in the present; and teach me the joy to be had there. They can't teach me how to connect with my own kind; for that, I need something much stronger. I think it would require a belief that I can *let* myself be happy, and create a need for the other person. I grew very self-sufficient to make it through what happened to me. Animals have taught me that vulnerability and trust can live in the same skin.

Over the last fifteen years, I've owned many horses, adopted some cats, and taken on even more dogs. In 1999, I found a dog whose breed remains one my favorites, a boxer. The little fellow whimpered from the desert outside my barn. I stood in the stallion pen working with Eros, and heard a faint sound somewhere on the other side of the fence. Over it, beyond a gang of cholla cactus, I could see a white ball on the red dirt. I went out on the desert to get to him. This boxer puppy suffered from a gunshot wound through the chest, someone's idea of sport maybe, or pure meanness. I picked him up, left my chores, and nestled him into the wide and worn seat of my big truck and took him to my horse vet, who was used to me showing up with strays in need of patching.

When I got him home after the ordeal to remove the shot, he was groggy, but responded with a grateful sweetness that I took to mean he knew that I had saved his life.

I did the honorable thing; I ran a notice in the Tucson paper to help his owners find him. But after a week of waiting for a response, and strangely dreaming over a few nights that his name began with "R," I decided he was fated to be mine and started calling him "Rocket."

In our single week together, Rocket and I developed a routine. I didn't have a partner then, but he made up for the company. He slept on my bed at night, and he spent all day at the barn with me as I taught riders and schooled horses. But on the eighth day I noticed a flyer on a corner streetlight pole in town.

"LOST DOG: White Boxer"

My chest tightened so that I could feel my heart beat hard under my skin. I loved him that much. I worked up the nerve to call the number, but the line was busy. I redialed for about an hour. Finally, a woman answered.

"I think I have your dog," I said without a hello, "He was shot, you know. And it's been a week now. Why haven't you been out looking for him?"

The lady, who I now know as Debbie, said that her family had been out every day of that week.

"Please can we come by and see if it's him?"

I told her where I lived and it seemed like only a minute later, they were in my driveway, seven of them: Debbie, her five daughters, and a son. They all piled out of the truck and went running over to the dog.

"Rocky! Rocky!" they all cried, so obviously grateful he was alive. Rocky, of all names. I started crying, too, to see that "my" dog was loved and missed and was going to leave me to go home. I told Debbie how to treat the wound that was now almost healed, and they left with the pup that I had grown to love in so short a time.

That night Debbie returned with some gifts for me to say thank you for taking care of Rocky. I felt like I'd lost a best friend. It's hard for me to explain why the openhearted love I feel from my animals so overwhelms me, and why losing one of them hurts so much; if you've felt it yourself you know. But the owner, who bred boxers, asked if I'd like to see Rocky in his home sometime, and see her breeding pair. When I did go, he recognized and greeted me instantly. Over a few more visits, the owner asked if I wanted a puppy, if she were to breed her dogs again.

Of course I did, and told her so, but I didn't trust that she meant it, and I'm impatient, so I started going to the Humane Society looking for a boxer to adopt. Once a week for two months, I strolled past the kennels of perfectly wonderful dogs and didn't find the soul I wanted to take home. The first week of month three, in block #8 was the dog I sought. CeeCee.

I asked a guy on the kennel staff if I could have her out in the "get-to-know" area. I sat on the picnic table there while he unsnapped her leash. She ran around the area once, then jumped on the table and put both her paws around my neck. Licking my face, our deal was made. I took her home that day and loved her every minute of every day I had with her. Like Rocky, she slept on my bed, and stayed outside with me even in the heat of the summer. She never left my side if she could help it.

After a year, Rocky's owner called again—they did have a litter of pups if I still wanted one. I picked a fawn male whom I named Boboli. Boboli and CeeCee were fast pals; she taught him how to jump my low arena fence, how to use the outside of the arena as a racetrack, how to sleep on the bed and push me to the very edge so they could have more room. It wasn't hard to move me.

CeeCee could jump over the low backyard fence when I got her, and she took a few desert forays that kept her away awhile. After her first year with me, she contracted Valley fever, a dirt-born virus that gets into the bones and causes intense pain. I did what I could, medicated her for three years, and watched her diet, but it's not something a dog always recovers from. I had to put her down in February of 2003. Boboli and I still miss her.

I tell this story because I want to consider how it is that I can still weep thinking about the animals I've loved and lost, but I don't always feel the same way about lost lovers. Of course I mourn them when I'm left, or when I leave. I would rather love and be loved by my human partners. But with an animal I am free to love without worry of rejection and in the full awareness of how glad he or she is that I am there.

Is it because my animals don't speak human? Is it speech, the easy words we give to one another that I don't trust? For me, I think part of the issue is that because the cost of speaking truthfully is so very high, if the person I'm talking to isn't listening, it's easy for me to think how much the effort of giving out my trust and hope to them will cost me.

Which brings me back to dressage. Some have likened watching dressage to watching grass grow. Or watching someone breathe or watching skating compulsories. The riding aids are subtle, the movements repetitive. Dull. But *doing* dressage, for me, is time-stopping. I am absorbed in the movement of and communication with the horse.

I've competed in horse shows and attended clinics with well-known trainers most of my life. When issues arise that the rider can't solve, or if the rider wants to move forward in a particular training method, the rider seeks a clinic and clinician to assist.

If I could turn the tables, then, there might be a clinic called the "Dressage of Human Relationships" for horses and their humans. This clinic would be taught by a horse. Instead of the humans working with a human clinician to solve a behavior in their horses or riding, the horses would bring their concerns about us to a four-legged equine expert, whose focus would be to put us rider-humans together into a temporary herd, so that we could listen to what our bodies and nonverbal energy says for us.

Horses are individuals, but they thrive in groups. They survive because they watch together for danger, and communicate clearly their intentions to each other. You scratch my withers, I'll scratch yours, so to speak. Our horses would attend such a clinic to solve the mystery of why humans put so much work into communicating but get such a small result. Talk, talk, talk. It seems the talk is the goal—not the listening. Not every human, in the horse's experience, hears a horse's subtle effort through the saddle and reins and acknowledges their attempt to say, "I'm listening, I think I understand what you want me to do." I'm certain we confound our horses sometimes. And it's not unthinkable that they watch our behavior with each other and wonder how we survive in our herds. My horse, Laramie, might enroll me in this clinic, despite a substantial waiting list. There would be so much interest in getting humans into these clinics that Laramie would be lucky to snag me a spot.

Let's imagine, now, that the clinician is a stoic Warmblood. This type of horse is usually heavy boned, and our bay-color expert is typical. LaGrande, my partner's diminutive, dusty brown Mustang mare, would have brought *her* to this event. Both Laramie and LaGrande truly want to understand why we can't speak plainly to each other about behavior that bothers each of us in the other. The stakes are high; one of us humans is sure the other will go silent, or one of us will walk away from the other. It's not clear to the horses why we do this. They hear the words, and can smell the tension that underlies the silences between words, and yet we pretend to be getting along and act as if there's really nothing that needs saying about any of this. It's a thing we two humans do, and the horses really don't get it. They would bite, kick, or isolate that herd member if she's being fractious—but they also know that the price of isolating a herd member could be that she does not survive out there alone some night. Do you really want your herd member to die? If you ignore a real issue and act like nothing's wrong, and so cause the isolation to continue, don't you get it that this might kill your herd mate? So there has to be an end to the punishment at some point and you must get that herd member to understand their behavior has to change and how in order for you to let them come back in.

My partner and I both are masterful in our own interactions with the horses we train, and our clients consider us gifted. But with each other, we struggle like so many other humans to get our interchanges right. I want everything from a relationship, know I cannot expect that, and want it anyway. And *right now.* My partner wants me to open up, to allow her access to my most private skeletons, but then it feels to me like she goes her own way in pursuit of individual plans and goals that leave me out. We both hurt each other. We're both guilty of lashing out in response to frustration and fear of losing each other. I want to say "Go to hell," but I don't believe speaking that plainly would have an effect. And, to turn my own tables, I don't really want to be that harsh, but I don't know how to say what I actually *do* want. I crave my partner's company but I don't want to be treated the
sometimes, an object for her to be angry at. I later reg
I treat my partner, too, when our relationship takes a

But I don't know how to stop. I feel weak and vulnerable because I can't tell what this other person thinks about me. I'm off balance. I can't seem to let go of my natural dread of the process of learning a new person, and trusting their intentions.

"I feel," Laramie tells the clinician, "that what they say to each other isn't half of what's going on, and despite the words, no one's listening to the message. Why don't they kick each other?"

The Warmblood walks up slowly, trying not to startle these two humans standing uneasily in the center of the arena. He tells the audience that he will allow us to communicate by body movement, or through facial expression, but we can't speak in *human*. I want to use words to explain what this feels like, but instead, I am allowed to only move closer to my partner. She looks into my eyes, and then as quickly turns away. I just want to run from her and this place.

We stand side by side now, the clinician's deep breathing all we hear. I note the difference in our sizes, comparing where her small-boned shoulder meets the tallness of mine. I smell the clean scent of her newly laundered shirt. She leans toward me. If I step back, she'll have to fall into the space I leave, catch herself before the fall, or turn altogether and go away from me. Each movement counts, and we both know it, yet we haven't exchanged a word.

The Warmblood turns his head in my direction, gazing with his large brown eyes from one of us to the other. He stretches out his neck. Without warning, he noses me so hard that I collapse against my partner's shoulder. Another shove and we both stumble back in response.

I am parched by the Tucson sun and irritated by this foreign communication.

The Warmblood casually moves in front of us, and where there was light, his body now creates a pool of shade. My partner steps into it. I follow. Degrees cooler here.

Apply lesson, wait for trust, give reward: The Warmblood shoulders me in passing, and I now stand my ground. My partner reaches me and stands, her shoulder to mine. I relax into the contact.

The other horses, who have been watching us from the rail, rotate their ears toward us and away. One yellowish dun mare snorts.

"Finally," she seems to be saying, maybe communicating the sentiments of the group. "Some of them take so long to come around."

His name was Cosmic, and he stood 17.3 hands, or 5 feet 9 inches at the top of his shoulder. Tall by any horse standards, this boy had the legs of a dancer. Gray in color, an extremely long head, and with black eyes that had a way of watching you wherever you moved, he had come up lame for my friend, his owner, in Kentucky. The lameness persisted, and finally, Dora's vet diagnosed navicular disease. It's an unspecified lameness that causes the front feet to be so tender that horses who have it almost seem to stand on tiptoe to avoid the pain. The treatment can range from doing nothing (pasture the horse forever) to the extreme of "nerving" or severing the nerves involved to alleviate the hurt, and then administering pain medication or blood thinners for the rest of the horse's life. Every owner fears hearing this diagnosis because the outcome is the same: *Your horse can no longer be ridden.*

Dora decided to have the nerving surgery performed, and Cosmic was no longer sore. But shortly thereafter, she called me.

"I can't keep him, Shelley," she said. "Can you please take him, if I send him to Tucson, and find him a home?" Dora was a doctor and had just entered a new residency, and had precious little free time to spend with Cosmic. His treatments and nerving surgery had also left her low on funds for his care. To let him just stand around if no one at the stable could even exercise him for her was a real issue.

"You want to ship him to me in Tucson, all the way from Kentucky? And he's not sound?"

"I know you'll find him the home he needs. And you'll get his training back together for me. He's sound now. He might remain that way."

Cosmic was seven years old and had been imported as a two-year-old from Germany. Westphalen by breed, he was destined to be someone's expensive dressage horse. Until this. But I knew that a diagnosis of navicular could also mean that the lameness, though persistent, wasn't something you could pinpoint. It could be his shoeing caused the pain. It could be the ground he was worked on. It could be navicular. I remembered that he had big good feet, and it's more likely for a horse with smaller feet in proportion to their body size to get navicular disease. I also knew that nerves can grow back—so the result of his nerving surgery might not be permanent. So many ifs.

Dora could be right that he was sound, and could remain so. I thought of the young woman in Washington—Sara—who was riding the loaned Arabian. If I could work out a price with Dora that would basically just cover Cosmic's transport, maybe Sara would be willing to take the horse with the understanding that he might work out, and might not. I'd have to also offer to take him back if not. But I knew that not all diagnoses of disaster hold water over time. I'd seen enough animals rally to a human's care to know anything is possible except in the most hopeless situations.

I called Leah in Washington and discussed pairing the gelding with Sara, but Sara was reluctant to commit. Maybe the owner of the Arabian would relent and sell her the mare if she realized Sara had another horse to take on. The owner was busy and knew Sara took good care of the mare. And wasn't this a lame horse? She wanted Meadow. I offered to ask the owner again for her, and the answer was still *no*.

Meanwhile, Dora called again—she would send him straight to Washington if that helped Sara decide—and he could return to Tucson if it didn't work. Sara still hedged because she knew the cost of treating a horse like this, if he required treatment again, could blast a hole in her finances, or mean he couldn't be ridden ever again.

So he came to me in Tucson instead. Cosmic arrived like a resigned prisoner. He'd lost weight in transport, and had a runny nose that indicated a possible respiratory infection, which may have kept him from eating on the trip. Horse haulers try to keep sick animals off the vans, but some slip through, and infect others. Cosmic lost his luck, if he had ever had any, by being stalled in transit next to a germy companion. The only strength left in him he reserved for refusing to back out of the van.

I put him in a stall, fed him, called my vet to check him, and settled in to providing a month of training on him and finding him a new home. But it was quickly apparent that training would be wishful thinking until he put more weight on. I didn't feel right having Dora pay me full board and training fees for a horse that might take six months just to be ready for enough work to make him show well for someone to adopt him.

My vet took a culture of the mucus from his nose, and called me three days later with the results. Pneumonia, and a fairly virulent strain. I had to put the entire barn on antibiotics. Three more days and he was still hardly eating.

Out of the blue, it seemed to me, Sara called and said she'd changed her mind about Cosmic. She wanted to negotiate with Dora and see if her original offer could stand, if he could be shipped to Washington. While Dora negotiated through me, Sara flew down to Tucson on a weekend to meet him.

She could stand under his throat and still have sunlight shine over the top of her head. We saddled him so she could take a short ride; I cautioned her that his hind end wasn't strong enough to support much in the way of work. Not until he got his weight back. As if he knew something was at stake, Cosmic went right into the work at hand. They moved well together, nothing forced or hard in their pairing. I wanted to know the instant she stepped off if she wanted him, but I couldn't push. Cosmic did what has become his trademark with Sara, touching the tip of his nose to her boot toe before and after a ride. She smiled at me.

After we put Cosmic back in his stall for the night, my partner and I took Sara out for dinner with a few of the clients from the barn.

In the back seat of the car Vicki, a client, nudged Sara.

"Well, what do you think?" Vicki said. Vicki was struggling to get to a place where she could communicate with her horse even a thimble-full of the way that Sara just had with Cosmic.

Sara sat quietly and avoided the question with a sly smile. "I want to call Leah first."

We pulled into the Krispy Kreme parking lot, bought a bag of hot doughnuts, and ate them all. We were all grateful it was Friday. The day was over, and we talked about restaurant choices. Sara borrowed my cell phone for the call to Washington. I hoped Cosmic was sold.

When we could tell she'd connected, we strained to listen in.

"Yes. Yes," she said. Then "I love him."

The next week, Cosmic began his trip up to Washington to live with Sara. The trip was long for him, and it would take almost a year for him to gain his weight back. But he bonded with the small herd there immediately, and always comes to Sara from wherever he is in the pasture when he sees her approach. No grudges for past lives in other barns, just unconditional devotion to this new human whose care he seeks like fresh grass. There will never be enough; he is always hungry.

So are *we* hungry, and thirsty, for the love of and intimacy with our human partners. I think abuse survivors, even those with a past different from mine, all crave an impossible level of intimacy from our loves. The easy connection for me is always with my animals. Much harder to reach to my partner and ask for what I need.

Perhaps the lesson I'm learning is that I can offer my human partner and friends something akin to Cosmic's patience with his world. I am driven forward away from the past, by a need to have someone love me. I believe we can create the need for another human, a space for them next to us in our herd. Without words, we can touch and sense that under our own skin flows a current of salty desire in the blood rivers of our bodies that has no language or need of it. We only have to get close enough to listen and receive sustenance from mutual need. The rest is instinct.

9
Passage

Winter stayed warmer than usual in 2003, and I took up the offer of good weather and started my seasonal spring tasks early. My young stallion Telluride, nearing three years old, was ready to be backed. This meant he was mature enough now for saddling, and the very gentle, slow process of a human mounting him by swinging a leg across his back, settling weight there gently, and then dismounting.

The weather was as perfect as it gets in the desert—golden and silky warm—exactly why those of us who choose to live here wait out the heat. I had the entire day to myself, no clients to teach or events to prepare for or barn errands to run. Jack, my longtime friend, had agreed to come out and help me. He'd grown up on a ranch in California, and scrappy guy that he was, he liked the notion of being up on Telly's back first, if my nerve failed me.

In my kitchen, I made my coffee and stood sipping at the counter, looking out my back window at the mountains. In the string of new moments with a horse you raise from a baby, you look forward to this one the most. But I was nervous about today. I ran my hand through my hair, and felt myself take in breath with the realization that it was finally happening, the first step in discovering the horse Telly would be. I also knew that it meant I would have to get serious about his training. Because of his size, I was giving him extra time to grow into his frame. The bigger horses can take longer to mature in body and in mind sometimes; I don't know why.

At over 18 hands, Telly was a Dutch Warmblood with four white socks and a full white blaze down a black-and-white face. As a pinto, he was marked with huge interconnecting patches of white and black hide. Telly was flashy. But he moved like a gangly teenager, long legs and young muscle, lacking the full bulk that would come with time and training. For all that presence and height and ability to smash something to smithereens if he wanted to, he was still startled by the smallest things. The instant appearance of a bird in his path, the garbage disposal truck grinding into the driveway, the roar of a motorcycle tearing through the sun on the road past my place. He'd shudder and dance, and raise his head as high as it could go. I stand five feet nine inches in my stocking feet, but when he was on alert with his head that high, I couldn't even reach his nose.

On the inside, Telly was younger—and older—than his three years. He didn't own all the experiences with humans he would have over time, that would make him the dressage horse and quiet guy I knew he would be. But he already possessed every one of the prey animal's primitive responses, fully intact and ready. Sometimes, in that moment of startling, he would stand as if rooted to the earth, still and tall, a complete receptor for something ahead or far outside himself. And then, just as suddenly, it would pass and he would visibly relax and be with me again. He would lower his head and chew, snort, and then let his breath out in a single long blow, as if expelling something he had sampled, found foreign, and did not want to keep deep within him.

I knew I would need to have my dressage saddle professionally adjusted to fit his back at some point, so that my aids would be clear and painless to him. The road to the higher movements such as *piaffe,* or trotting almost in place, and *le passage*, or the intensely collected trot that looks like floating, would be long and slow. But today, as I gently led him to the mounting block in the round pen, my saddle was just a surface to hold human weight.

Jack watched, standing short and durable in his worn dusty boots and faded Levis. I felt comforted by his presence. He is always willing to help me out, fixing a tractor or mending a fence. He is the person in my horse life who takes care of me around the edges, knowing I don't know what to do with too much personal attention, but giving just enough and in ways that matter—fiddling with my failed equipment or getting my ancient tractor "Miss Olivia" tuned, or rehanging a gate that one of the horses had bent. He knows I can't take care of those things very easily by myself. No matter how long you live alone, and how self-sufficient you are, you never get used to having only one pair of hands.

I led Telly closer to the mounting block. It had homemade steps topped with a wide flat platform. It was tall so that I could easily step up on the bigger horses I trained. As we reached the block, Telly's body tensed and his muscles hardened under his skin. To a horse, anything can be a predator, even a mounting block. I calmed him with my voice, gently urged him to take a step laterally, and another, until he stood parallel to the block. As quietly as I could manage, I took the first step up, then the second. I patted his rump, then the saddle, and worked forward to run my hand down his neck. *It's ooh-kaay...good Telly...easy. It's okay.* Now I lightly thumped the saddle with the flat of my hand, which caused him to step away. I got off the block, and we walked together around the circumference of the pen, returning again to the center and the block. We had done this several times over the past few weeks to prepare, but no matter, it really was up to Telly to invite me into his fear by yielding with his body, almost like being willing to give up a bit of his life for me, in his own time. As much as he trusted me to feed him and brush him and be with him, he had no experience that could have prepared him to trust something, *someone*, on his back. Anything could happen. This was his instinct.

My grandfather damaged me sexually and scarred me emotionally. But whether I call it a human survival instinct or just my need to physically break through the extreme loneliness that camps out at the border-crossing of my skin, sex is still important to me. Touch and love are vital to me. And finding a way to cross the empty zone at the border to a new country where I can trust a partner has taken me years of talking and crying and trying harder and being one person here and another there until I can sometimes finally, *finally* get it right in myself and with another.

I've had a few partners over thirty years. Some seemed right and we lasted awhile, others were emotionally terrorizing. I also brought my own baggage that could be hard for a partner to comprehend. I know I always played a part in the endings. My journey to reach a new country of real trust can take me back, more often than not, to a familiar and battered place in myself that is just big enough for only one inhabitant—me. I always return here far lonelier and thirstier for love than when I left.

As an adult, I've unconsciously chosen relationships in which I could become a victim. I chose partners who would never be available to me in any permanent way, or from whom I withheld myself sexually, feeling it wasn't safe for me to stay present. I have tried to heal and get love in ways that reflected the feeling I had on the inside—that I never really deserved love. I deserved whatever I got.

But instinct is powerful, and mine to survive forced me to find ways to get better. Like a trapped and wild horse, I felt I had two elemental choices. I could break my neck going through the fence line that enclosed my freedom, or find a way to stay and survive in new circumstances. Finally, just surviving wasn't enough. I needed to be loved and to thrive just as much as I needed to get by.

If I pour water on a hard piece of desert quartz, and watch it run off, I can pretend the rock isn't changing, trying to take in that water one molecule at a time. But it has to be changing. Over time, the rock will erode so it can let the water in, and change. It will become sand, and in a rainstorm be lifted and married to the water that rushes through—not like it was, but as something new. Maybe the first grains in a ripple of a river bottom. Over time, I slowly told my stories, first to therapists, then to a few very caring friends, and always to my horses when I rode or worked around them. My horses listen well, especially to body language and the scent of emotions, and on more than one occasion, to some subtle things humans just can't bear to hear. And so I changed, one cell at a time. I tried to take myself apart, and put myself back together somehow in the human community around me.

In January of 2003, for the first time in more years than I care to remember, I knew that what I truly wanted was a real relationship with one person who would stay. I wanted to breathe with another human being. At the edge of my personal desert, I stood anxious, waiting to cross to a horizon I could only barely see.

I paused on the mounting block beside Telly. Telluride is a horse mountain, strong and fine. Calm and soft-eyed, he seemed ready for the moment at hand.

Horses remember every interaction with us. It would be so easy for me to screw this up. I quietly took the reins into one gloved hand, patted the saddle leather from pommel to cantle, front to back, and then smoothed my palm over his rump. I gently positioned my left foot in the center of the stirrup iron. I was aware that I was holding my breath, and straightened myself so I could let it out and inhale deeply, trying to let go of my own fear. Both his and my own safety mattered so much to me. We could lose a lot in a split second, all of it about trust. I willed myself steady and calm, filling my lungs with warm January air. I leaned into his side and rested my chest over the saddle's seat so he could feel some of my weight on him before I ever stepped up. I waited a single breath, only long enough for him to feel the pressing of my body, and then I pulled back.

He stood like a statue. His eye held a curious light, and his nostrils flared as if tasting a new scent. If a horse can have an expression on his face, Telly's was one of disbelief and wonder that the person who stood beside him, who brushed him and fed him, could have been on his back.

A few months before this moment on Telly, still a single woman, I was talking to a dear friend in her office, telling her how much I needed to see if my work on myself had progressed. Was I healed yet, any nearer to whole? Was it enough to share with someone?

"I need to be in a relationship." I said. "There's no other way I'll know what I'm like now."

"Oh you have many relationships, Shelley," she answered casually, leaning back in her chair. But as she watched my sun-marked face I saw in her eyes a look of growing concern and alertness. She knew me well, she knew the effects of my past, and how far I would sink into myself if—in my mind—I encountered the predator at my bedside, no matter who was really with me.

"You have relationships with the clients you meet every day," she said. "You spend weekends out of town with them and with friends at dressage shows. All this is good. You're healing, you're doing really well. You haven't broken apart in a very long time. Why risk it?"

I could imagine that she worried and hoped, in equal parts, that I didn't head into another relationship that would fail. I had internalized patterns of abuse by others so deeply that I could, and did, abuse myself without them.

"I know, and I understand what you're saying, but I've worked so hard. I'm honorable with the people around me. I feel different. I'm strong because I'm speaking up about it all. I'm starting to see my grandfather for what he was—a sick, sad old man taking his wants and frustrations out on someone who couldn't fight back or tell about it. But until I'm in a sexual relationship that works, that's safe, I won't have all of myself back. I can't be certain I'm really healing. Hoping that I might have moved on from my abuse isn't proof that I have."

My friend and I both knew it was true.

In the strangely warm Tucson winter, I met my partner through my friend. With this person, something felt very different in me. I could be present through all my fear, panic, and hope, even enough to flirt and be myself. Clear in my desire, I was trusting and sexual, and my partner returned this in kind. But despite what felt strongest in me, I still worried my partner would leave me. I might be too intense and overwhelm her, or maybe I would screw this up in another way. Then I would become the victim. I knew I was trusting from a place inside that was totally vulnerable and raw. Sometimes I could hardly breathe through it all. But I wanted desperately to keep going. I wanted to be okay with my partner.

But for the first time in a relationship, I reached out and I didn't run away. I wrote in my journal when I was scared, telling myself a story of the good that comes from staying present just one moment longer than what I thought I could stand, even when I couldn't hold on to myself, and trying to believe this could all work.

And yet the thing that mattered most, what I wanted worse than anything I have ever wanted in my life, I found I still could not give. In sex, I couldn't risk giving up all of my control to my partner. I simply knew I couldn't.

By the time I was twelve years old, I was old enough and fast enough so that my grandfather couldn't catch me any longer to have sex with me. As a result, my ten years of abuse in his hands and by his mouth ended. Now forty-two, I still would not allow myself to be *caught*, nor would I let anyone ever have me completely or satisfy me completely. My fear of losing control ran too deep, and when I got to that vulnerable point in sex, I could feel myself hiding at the very bottom of my humanity—naked, two years old, fondled by a man I should have been able to trust, hurting, and angry. It didn't matter if the person with me wasn't him, didn't look like him or smell like him. I got scared.

I was certain that if I told my partner this story, everything would break with us, and that the pieces wouldn't be able to be recast as something good. If I risked letting go of all of the worry and pain and just tried to believe I *might* be okay, I would disintegrate into an echo of myself. So I refused to take the step.

All of this was suddenly back in my thoughts as I worked with Telly and Jack.

Telluride is the offspring of Eros, a Dutch Warmblood stallion I once owned, and Laramie, my Grand Prix dressage mare. Telly was born in my barn on April 28, 2000, the first foal for me in the new millennium. He was a piece of hope made solid for the future. I loved him instantly, as we do with the young in our care. I needed Telly to become vulnerable and trust me for this backing to succeed. How could I ask him something that I wouldn't do? To be vulnerable and let go?

Telly's conception and birth run contrary to how I handled my clients' mares. I had assisted at the foaling of many maiden mares, which are mares that have never had a baby, and thought because of my experience I could as easily make it through the emotions of watching my own mare's pregnancy. But I discovered as soon as she was pregnant just how much Laramie meant to me. I foolishly let myself read about all the things that can go wrong in foaling, and worried myself straight into nightmares of loss and disaster. I knew my instincts with horses and foaling were keen, that I could respond quickly and appropriately at the first sign of trouble with a foal. But I also suspected that because I was growing afraid of losing her, and because a difficult birth might mean a choice between mare and foal, that I might lose my nimble reactions and calm reserve right when I needed it most.

Horses carry foals for eleven months. I continued to ride Laramie until, at nine and a half months, she was just too big to get a saddle and girth around. In her eighth month, a well-known trainer came to town, and I decided to ride in the clinic she held. Tucson is a small town by most measures, so when a trainer with a well-known name in the dressage world comes to town, the dressage community inevitably all turns out to watch the riders and horses.

My legs draped over the big curves of Laramie's sides as I walked her into the arena where the trainer stood waiting for us. It seemed all I did was enter that arena and the trainer started to bark instructions at me that felt pointed and personal. She had it in for me. I don't know what triggered the instructor to use my ride as the example for everything that a rider could do wrong, but she chose me, and Laramie and I were in for trouble.

She asked me to trot, and after a few strides pointed out to the clinic attendees, many of them people I competed with, how we were not straight, or collected, or basically anything.

"This is what not to look for in a horse and rider," she said, and picked at my seat and hands and Laramie's movement with every word.

For forty-five minutes I sat Laramie's big, heavy-bellied trot as the instructor ordered one high-level movement after another, all interlaced with acid commentary. I trotted on and on. I was paralyzed by my embarrassment for both of us, and appalled and ashamed as we moved together because I couldn't make myself speak up and stop the lesson.

Panic coiled so tight in my chest that I was spring-loaded for flight. Laramie sensed my tension through my seat and hands, and I could tell she was wondering what on earth was happening to both of us. I wanted the ground to open and swallow me and Laramie whole, never to be seen above earth again. I was surely pushing her where I shouldn't, and delivering nothing as a rider. She was having to carry me, and this foal, without release from the tension in my body and hers.

Suddenly, without warning and feeling like something snapped inside her, I noticed that something recoiled sharply in her belly and back, directly under my seat. I knew something had happened inside her body. In just two more strides I could feel that she had pulled a groin muscle. But because she was a strong mare and a professional athlete, and had gotten no signal to stop from me, she kept going. I kept riding too, knowing full well I should have stopped immediately. We finished the lesson. I now felt like a worm, spineless and low, in the saddle of a majestic, very pregnant, and honorable mare and friend. I had let her down so severely I could barely acknowledge it to myself.

Don't tell, I heard in my head. *This is bad, but if you tell it will all get worse. Because you should know better. Because you are her caretaker. Because you should have spoken up and stopped everything. Now if you tell they will know you rode on and did nothing, nothing at all. If you tell you will die and you deserve it.*

I led her back to my trailer. *If you tell, you'll die.* This time the voice in my head meant my reputation; that I had risked hurting my own horse for what? How could I have done that? How could I advocate for me needing care when I couldn't take this one life that mattered so much to me and prevent this pain? Now, it was two lives. I was doubly guilty.

I fell in on myself with shame. I didn't ride Laramie or my clients' horses for days afterward. I made excuses for lessons I should have gone to teach and let my calls pile up in voicemail. I had put my mare and the foal I wanted so desperately in grave danger. I wasn't a professional. I felt like a fraud.

I cried for her, for the foal, and just as much for myself.

I had a dream that recurred night after night, well before Telluride was ever born.

It always started this way...

I stand in the coolness of my barn, a breeze drying my face. I have been crying and feel emptied and without any will to care about anything. Sounds reach me—traffic from the nearby road, the buzz of heat and insects, horses snorting and shuffling nearby in soft dirt.

A foal steps close to my side—Telly—I know it is him. He is fresh and wet from his birthing. He stretches his tiny nose oh so tentatively to me. His face shines sharp black and crisp white, a pinto. I see four white socks, and want to stroke the perfect blaze of white down his small head. I realize as I dream on that he has *not* been born yet, that I am really in Telluride's dream as he sleeps in Laramie's womb. Or maybe, our dreams have interlaced, so that we can meet here in surreal time in the desert of wanting desperately to be alive. If we want hard enough for each other, we can stay present here and see each other.

I want to press my lips to the brow over his soft chocolate eyes, and touch his whiskered velvety muzzle. Again, he stretches his nose to me and barely touches my hand, and in that very instant, he vanishes as if he is only a magician's trick. My gloved hand touches only air. I reach up to my face to brush salt tears that become diamonds as they drop from my eyes and lips to sparkle at my feet.

When Telly finally arrived looking exactly as he had in my dreams, I wasn't surprised by his markings. We recognized each other by sight.

In the tenth month of Laramie's term, in late March or early April of 2000, I started checking on her at least two or three times each night. I was edgy from lack of sleep and stress, and my bones ached from the tension my muscles applied to them to keep me going when I was so tired.

In mid-April, I moved out to the barn to sleep with my big girl. I'd called Marnie, my vet, to update her on Laramie's progress and told her I knew for sure the foal would come soon. I made a decent bed outside of Laramie's stall from a sleeping bag and foam pad, and gave my two dogs the choice of where to hang out, inside the house or with me in the barn at night. My young boxer chose to look out for me; my older boxer stayed inside to guard the house. My demons were kept at bay in both places by my faithful dogs.

Boboli and I slept well in the desert night. Laramie just paced.

On April 28, nearing five o'clock in the evening, Laramie circled her stall with a fresh anxiety. Her stools were loose. I stroked her neck to try and calm her as I called the vet on my cell phone. *There, Laramie. Easy big girl.*

"I am positive, Laramie is ready to foal," I told Marnie as soon as she answered.

"Call me when you're really sure," Marnie said. "You know how long this can take. I have several calls left—I'll be there as soon as I can. I promise. We have time."

"Look, I *am* sure—don't be long." I ended the call impatiently. *Just get here damn it*, I thought.

Within the hour, Laramie's water had broken. She was now completely terrified of the changes taking place in her, and clearly didn't like her body betraying her. She slumped to the floor of her stall in agony. She pushed once, twice. She gave me a look, female to female, that said plainly, *help me.*

As automatically as breathing, I had grabbed the bottle of Betadine antiseptic scrub and poured the rusty-colored liquid over the lengths of my arms and down to my hands and palms. Then I reached my arm in through her vagina to her uterus. I felt the perfect presentation for birth of the foal—hoof, nose, hoof, pointed down and ready. In my mind, I could see the exactness of the foal, Telly, who had visited me in the dream. It would be a white hoof, a pink nose, and a white hoof.

But now I could tell Laramie really wasn't pushing anymore. It happened so quickly, her change to lethargy, and I knew it wasn't going to change back. Taking a deep breath and hoping for enough strength, I gently and firmly pulled Telluride out of his mother. He slid to the ground with a wet thump. Laramie, lifting her head, nickered instantly.

I knew my job was over—I needed to step out and let them bond. Laramie confirmed this by looking at me with an expression in her eyes that said this was private, so move along.

I was standing outside the stall, rubbing my hands on my jeans. I looked up to see my client Jean had arrived.

"Tell me! Filly or colt?" she whispered as if we were in a maternity ward.

I stopped and stared blankly.

"You know I didn't check. Colt. I'm pretty sure," I said, dazed.

I started to laugh as she hugged me and I knew it didn't matter if my dream colt actually was a filly; my mare and new foal were alive, okay, and resting. I was relieved and blessed. I called Marnie back to tell her that I had been right, but that everything was in hand, and if she would drop by as soon as she could to check out the foal, I'd be grateful.

I settled on the pad outside the stall door and fell asleep. When I woke, two hours had passed and I thought that I had given Laramie and the baby enough time to be up and about. I stretched, rose, and slowly rolled the stall door open. Laramie struggled to her feet with a grunt. Telluride, perfect little horse, wobbled on his black and white bony legs.

I wanted to steady him and moved carefully forward. Laramie's expelled placenta had made the stall floor slick, and just as I reached Telly, my boot slipped in it and I lost my balance, bumping hard into Telly. The foal lost his own footing, and flipped onto his back and hit his head on the stall wall. Extending my hand to right him and check his head, he immediately recoiled from my touch as if it were again the unseen force that had thrust his small body backward. He didn't trust me. For months to come he would react this way to my touch.

We can lose something this valuable with a simple misstep.

Now I must tell you an even harder story. Understand that it is difficult and risky for me to relate something so personal about me in this way to you. But I know that I risk more by not telling you. I want to open the door to my story for you, so that maybe if you also suffer in a place guarded and frightening and dread looking closely at what has maybe happened to you, the telling of my own truth can help us both out into a lighter place. I tell my story tentatively, but with hope. I will wash my story in the velvet moon of a desert night—bright enough so that you can see the sand, the cholla, the tiny creatures, and the wariness of my heart, yet dark enough, I promise, to keep our secrets safe.

Because my grandfather used me for his own sexual fulfillment, and I had nowhere to run, I learned to dissociate at times during sex. I can't say where I go, but in that moment when I should give myself to my lover, I either carefully take myself away physically so that I barely feel my partner's touch, or I emotionally rise out of myself and leave in spirit.

Despite my years of trying to change this behavior, and having found a new love who meant so much to me, I found that I was still unwilling to give up the final piece of myself to sexual intimacy that would allow me to stay present and really feel. Or was I incapable because of what had happened in my past?

It is crippling to refrain from engaging your heart, mind, and body as one. But this is exactly what I did.

My new love wanted to be my life partner, not just a lover, and offered me strength and attention. And asked me this question: Why couldn't I let go, trust, and give over this piece of myself?

We talked over many days, and I explained how I got to this protected place where I held myself safe against everyone, never letting anyone in to further damage my broken heart. I couldn't risk it. Yet risking the loss of my partner human felt far graver to me. I hurt just thinking about my partner's possible absence. I had to try and give what I was asked for. My partner wanted to help, to take me, and show me that I could still remain whole. I wanted to believe her.

A night of candles and soft liquid music.

I couldn't think about horses or worries or tomorrow. I was fully in this moment and our intertwining happened gently, an evening samba hip to hip. Moments stilled and tightened to a single point, when she asked me to let go, to give myself up, and surrender what happened to my body.

I couldn't breathe through my heartbeats. My chest would surely explode, and my heart would be left like an empty sack. I did and did not want to lose myself to this person whom I wanted desperately to trust. *Take me, then, hold me. Please. I give this to you.*

It happened without warning. I felt myself slip through my skin like vapor and float far above the two of us. The feeling of leaving was irresistible and satisfying. As nearly as I can describe it, I softly left the present Shelley in that room and entered a version of me from an earlier place in my life, when I was two years old and safe, whole before abuse, held and warm where no hurt could come. It felt so calming to sink into this familiar darkness so thick that my eyes closed under the weight. I couldn't hear or feel the body I left behind.

I either slept or had passed out; I don't know for sure. Mere minutes passed on the clock face on the nightstand, but to my partner, my abandonment felt like forever and she was very angry.

I returned from vapor to body and fell hard back into myself. I was disoriented. I didn't know where I had gone or how long I had been there. My partner was furious. I didn't know what to do or have words to explain it.

"Wasn't I good enough to keep you awake and with me? Is there something so very wrong with me? What is the point of this if you leave me?" she said.

Hurt filled the room.

For hours, we fought and talked and struggled to make clear to each other what our needs were, what might have happened. I groped for an explanation.

"Something is wrong with me," I said. Far worse, I thought, I'll lose this person whom I've finally, at long last, found, if I can't explain. My grandfather, a ghost in this bed with us, had sucked me dry as desert bone.

I cried for hours, thoroughly disgusted with myself.

"I need to talk to someone who can help, who knows about sexual abuse," I finally said. "That's what this is about. I can't do this anymore. I'll never be normal. Something is so very wrong with me."

I explained my life, into the small night hours, and tried hard to tell her where I'd come from.

"It *is* about my childhood, not about you. This dissociation is comforting to me. It's like I'm suddenly two years old and have no language to fight and must find the only place that is safe, which means I have to leave myself, because there is nowhere else I can go except out of my body. It's painful to me, too. How could I have let this happen to me now? How could I leave the one person I've dedicated so much time and love to? Do you think I want to? How could I leave you if I could control it? Don't you think I care enough about you to stay present if I could?"

The same old questions that haunted me day after month after year: How could I move forward into something new with this past cinched tight around my throat?

Finally, all our talking finished, my partner quietly crossed the room, sat beside me, and stroked my cheek and neck. I swallowed a small knot of memory from my childhood that had lodged in my throat. That memory of my abuse tasted bitter. I didn't want any more to even be in my life, now, abusing myself through this memory, over and over and over. Thirsty to death and finally arriving at water through a relationship, I wanted to stretch my cupped palm and drink deeply from my partner's care, but I could take only the smallest sip.

The time between one swallow and the next can be very long. I struggled to take in enough to sustain me.

I'm still healing, but in the end, my partner and I had to take separate paths through our own personal deserts. We just couldn't give enough of ourselves.

I believe I will be present for the right person some day, but for now, I want to be present for myself. It's very hard work for me.

I tell you this story not for my healing only, or to ask for any sympathy, but maybe by example to give you a little heart and courage to speak your own story. It doesn't matter quite as much as you think who you tell it to. You might have to tell it many times, as you remember it, and as you can, to many different people. I remind myself that I am practicing for the time when the right person is there to listen. Nothing will ever be as important to your own safety or mine as remembering, and telling, your story.

My grandfather has been dead a long time. Now, and only when I think about it too much, I do still have those moments of panic around the issue of incest. I'm sad for that man who would take a child for his partner in sex, whose grandchildren hated him. Helpless and lost in his behavior and desires, he must have lacked the will to find anyone who could help. Or maybe he didn't realize he himself had made the very landscape he was so lost in.

After Telly fell as a foal, he would recoil or shy whenever I tried to touch his head to brush or bridle him. We worked steadily and long to make it okay for me to enter his space there and soothe him.

Today, before I lifted the saddle onto his back, I understood the courage it took for him to let me approach and do this. What happened between Telly and me was not abuse, but he has a past experience with me that hurt, is here, and still feels real to him. We could go around it or through it. Telly owned the answer.

I stood back a small distance away after Jack took Telly's reins from me. His turn. He patted the silky black-and-white hide, touched the little white "vee" in the black pattern on his neck muscle, and Telly chewed. Contentment. I waited far enough away from Telly's side to safely jump back if I needed to, but remained close enough to comfort my colt.

Jack swung a leg over Telly's back and lightly settled in the saddle. Telly stayed calm. I thought, *well then, Jack is a different person. Telly has no issues with him.*

Suddenly, fear made Telly drop his back away from Jack's weight. Jack lifted himself off and swung down with the grace of a cat.

Telly wasn't sure what had happened to make the threat come and then go, but he had survived it. Like when a cloud passes across the sun and you feel chilled and then warm again, he seemed to sense that he could trust this experience just a little because it had come and then evaporated and he was still okay.

We would work like this for days, so many repetitions of this little act. No more than this, and then a bit more, until finally, that union of beings trying to understand each other's language would begin. I was anxious and hopeful for Telly and for me. We each had a kind of healing to do. A friend once said to me, "Forgiveness is letting go of the wish for a different past." If that's true, then I think trust is knowing that the present is not only the past retold, but finally, forgiven.

10
Serpentine

I want to tell you a story about losing—and recovering—my horse Telluride.

He will likely never be a dressage horse. But Telly has shown me that what we lose can define us. In fact, sometimes, the loss is the only thing that makes a transformation possible.

When something happens to me that seems wrong, maybe bad, maybe life threatening, I tend to see only the negative and say *why me*. Probably, we all do. Many times, no answer satisfies me. When I watch a desert snake traveling in the dirt, I notice how it winds where it wants to go, and in the next movement turns back to approach where it has been. That feels like my life. I move forward, then back, heal, get injured, and keep winding on, going almost nowhere at all. But I know the snake moves forward, despite the recoil of her path, and so maybe I do too. What I learned through Telly is that loss prepares each of us to become something different, if we are open to the challenge.

My grandfather should never have abused me, and I shouldn't be scared by the landscape of intimacy. I want to feel safe with my own human kind. I lost a lot of myself. In what I lost of Telly, I might have seen an omen of what I would lose in my own life. In the way he came back to me, I have no doubt the lesson was about something else entirely.

In early 2004, my life came looking for me. Telluride, the horse I had seen in my dreams before his birth, and in whom I placed so much hope as my ultimate dressage mount, started behaving strangely. He would kick out with his hind leg suddenly and without warning, as if experiencing a painful cramp. I thought about calling the vet, but he was sound otherwise. And sometimes when in your soul you know *this* thing is *very* serious, you do just the opposite of what you should—you hunker down and try to convince yourself that your intuition, please, just this once, is absolutely wrong. You pretend and go on, for awhile.

Telly was four years old. I had delayed his training longer than usual and had not taught him much beyond the basics of walking and trotting on a line in a circle around me. I could, and did ride him at the walk, but I hung back because of this random, unpredictable behavior. I worried that he would throw me—and at 18.2 hands, the ground is a long way from the saddle. I am my sole source of income—employer and employee. So if I get hurt, it's dire. By the time Telly's hind-leg behavior was becoming more frequent, I was also seeing the odds increase that I *would* get hurt.

I made two decisions. First, I would send Telly to another trainer who came highly recommended by colleagues. I cried for days over this, because I worry about each and every one of my animals when they're out of my sight, and felt mostly like I was letting Telly down by not doing this work myself. Second, I would find a way to continue my work with horses in the therapy field. Now in my mid-forties, the price of a broken bone is more than the hospital bill. Psychologically, I was becoming the middle-aged woman afraid of the big fall. It creeps in a little at a time, this sense that you've cheated the dirt one too many times. My sun-browned cheek bears a white scar that covers a nerve that can sing sharp pain through my day—the result of a long-ago ride when a rein broke, the horse ran off and bucked, and I flew face first into contact with hoof and fence. My nose was crushed, and my cheek near my eye was peeled back like mango skin. The emergency surgery to fix the damage was very badly done, and the subsequent operations never really got my face right. But the white scar reminds me daily that there is always a price for living your life. Some days I don't see the scar. Other days, it is all I see. On those days, I worry about falling.

I wasn't just losing my courage to ride the young horses. It was more. I was changing inside. I wanted to do more than just work at the surface of my life. I wanted to make some difference to someone else with what I had learned with my horses. That piece of me screamed to be given a chance.

I had thought about my work with Sierra Tucson so many times over many years, and always sought out others who were interested in horses as a part of a healing therapy. A decade ago I had gotten involved with my friend Linda Kohanov and a circle of other colleagues. We collaborated on the beginnings of a way of being with and training horses that fostered emotional growth for the humans, and respect for the animals. Linda would go on and nurture her dream into the Epona Center outside of Tucson. I stayed in touch with Linda as I continued my work in dressage.

In December of 2004, in addition to sending Telly to a trainer for a month of evaluation, I applied for and started in an equine apprenticeship in Linda's Epona Center, now a mature collective of educators, counselors, physical therapists, and riding instructors exploring the healing potential of horse-human relationships. Linda, my longtime friend, was surprised at this turn in my life, and delighted to see me apply.

I was losing an enormous piece of myself, stepping outside the profession of dressage work. I had taught riding and competed in Tucson for twenty years, and had run my life by the calendar of show seasons and client horses arriving for training. Now I was taking my life into work with people who knew how the horse-human bond can change us. Could I make a difference? Would it be right for me?

My new apprenticeship would be another challenge. School, in whatever form, frightens me because I had let the feeling that I was "stupid" and "not a good student" sink deep into my way of being. Remember I fled school and have lived in the horse world ever since. I doubted my ability to get through the courses.

During the time of this apprenticeship year, for one intensive week every three months, the members of my group and I would gather at Linda's facility outside of Tucson. We immersed ourselves in horse-human therapies, readings, writings, speakers, practices, and finally, we learned to conduct our own workshops. We were encouraged to look carefully at what horses can teach about authentic behavior and true responses to situations emotional and physical. At the end of each of these weeks, I was emotionally spent and raw, but tremendously awake. I was reconnecting in the work I did here. People who came to work the horses began to find ways to apply what they'd learned to behavior in their lives. I felt challenged by my new work, and wanted more.

Because I was a horse trainer, and I lived nearby in Tucson, Linda also hired me during this time to work with her horses. She has an elderly and beloved black Arabian stallion named Merlin, a black Arabian mare named Rasa, and their very small young son, a black Arabian stallion named Spirit who was now three years old. Spirit is the sole survivor of a pair of twin black foals. These members of Linda's therapy herd were also her spiritual companions.

A couple of days each week, I traveled to her facility and worked the three horses, one after the other, in a round pen. After a short time, I sensed they were bored with human instructions—walk, trot, canter, *whoa*—and remembered what Chuck Grant had shown me about horse tricks. The intelligence in these Arabian horses was easy to see, and I felt they wanted to *do* something to interact with me. The tricks—standing on a drum like an elephant, stepping across a plank balanced like a seesaw on a log, bowing—were easy enough to teach.

We started with the "circus drum." Moving freely around me in the round pen, I taught each one how to approach me, how to come forward and stand on a mounting block, and how to place first one front hoof on the lowest step, and then the other hoof. Gradually each horse would climb the steps to place both front hooves on the top step, standing tall and obviously pleased with the achievement, waiting for treats.

Spirit, the young stallion, eclipsed Merlin in his quick understanding of what I wanted him to do, and I nicknamed him "the horse genius." It wasn't long before he would watch for my truck pulling in to Linda's, and would paw at his paddock gate, ready and waiting. On the way in to the facility one morning, I thought it would be something to see the father and son doing the same routine side by side.

Walking to their pens, I took both stallions, and put them into the round pen. First they needed to learn to be with each other in the same space. We practiced until I could ask them both to respond to my voice commands and not run wild around me. Over the next mornings, I worked them together until they would stand, side by side, front feet on a pair of mounting blocks, like ebony bookends in the sun. Linda watched from the deck of her nearby house.

A few days later, she took me aside and asked if I could introduce Rasa into this picture. Two stallions, okay. But add a mare? Let's say I was skeptical. I brought Rasa in and we began. With Linda's belief in her herd, and with time and much repetition, we got a family of horses together all standing on their blocks—mare, stallion, and son stallion. This would never happen without human intervention, and it's reasonable to say that I was asking for a movement that was highly rewarded by treats, and horses are motivated by a good snack. But it would not happen at all without the horses being patient and trusting of me, and somehow being willing to work together. I gave them a challenge; they accepted. Why? They changed the way they would normally behave in a herd because I think they enjoyed learning this odd new way to communicate with me. Essentially, they let me *lead* their herd to see if I could. Mutual respect? Simple animal training? Or human-horse relating? Whatever I might call it, I was honored at their acceptance and trying.

Back at home, Telly's first month with the new trainer was nearly over, and he wasn't better. The head trainer didn't think he'd ever make a trustworthy mount. They had tried, he said, but Telly had bucked his own private rodeo out there. He lightly recommended that I might want to consider selling him for just that, a rodeo string. With his size and energy, he could really be something. I was appalled and devastated that I had let Telly down in this way. He wasn't a rodeo horse. I had failed him. I took it all back onto myself because I should have been the one to do this work with him. I should not have been afraid. Now he would be even less trusting of me, and I had his newly learned bucking behavior to deal with—which might really get me hurt. I trailered him home the next day, ashamed of myself and sad. Telly stepped off the trailer and I led him back to his paddock where his mother, Laramie, waited to greet him. They nuzzled each other, blew breath in contentment, and Telly calmly returned to the life of standing about that he knew so well.

A few days passed, and I continued to travel to work with Linda's three horses, trying to deal with this disappointment I felt in myself. On my way home one evening, my friend Lee called to check on Telly and me. I told her what the result of his training had been, and she offered on the spot to take him to her barn and try to get him going. She said she always wanted to try to start a young horse, that she liked Telly, and that she felt she was up to the work.

I wanted to do right by Telly, to give him another chance, and I couldn't do it myself. So I accepted her offer.

Lee began working with Telly and managed to move him along gently and well, so that he was trotting calmly with her in the saddle. They were just beginning to canter. But within his first few weeks at her barn, he became lame without warning, and now couldn't be ridden. When I visited, I found him standing tall and alone in a side paddock. I imagined he waited stoically for something, anything at all, to change in his day.

"How's his tricky fin?" I asked Lee when she came out to talk with me. I called his rear leg jerking his "tricky fin," because Telly reminded me of Nemo, the little fish in the movie *Finding Nemo* not only because of his odd "fin," but because like Nemo, he'd somehow gotten lost in a current and needed to get back home. Due to the events in my life, he wasn't on the road to a top-level dressage horse's career anymore. He was adrift in a sea of jerking movements and humans who walked away from him, scratching their heads and shrugging shoulders, as if to say, *He sure is beautiful. Too bad you can't ride him.*

"His leg isn't great, but I work around it," she said. "Have you had it checked?"

"Not yet."

I couldn't say anything more to her about it. I know I was waiting foolishly for this to miraculously go away, and I also know miracles, like water, are spare in my desert. I took Telly home.

By June, 2005 I finally asked a vet to look at Telly. For months now, I had watched as Telly's odd movements got worse. Now when he even lowered his head to the ground to eat his hay, or anytime I worked him on a circle at the end of a line, he would jerk the leg out as if in a spasm. I could no longer pretend this would heal itself. As a horse professional, I would have advised a client to call for a consult immediately if this had been their horse. But there are times when you don't want to know something as badly as you might otherwise, because it's not going to end well. I knew for sure that I wasn't ready to let go of this dream called Telly. Not yet.

I had a vet with a horse in my training, and in talking to her about Telly, she offered to do a neurological exam. While I held his lead rope, the vet crossed Telly's front legs easily. He was fine, and snuffled my collar from his great height as if to say, *What's this new game about?* But when we tried to get him to cross his back legs, he started to experience a seizure.

"I can't tell without additional tests," the vet said, "but I do think you should take him to Arizona Equine for a head and neck x-ray. It's not good. It could be a pinched nerve in his neck, it could be Wobblers."

Wobbler syndrome can refer to several disease states in a horse. The most common, cervical vertebral malformation, is characterized by a badly formed or compressed spinal cord. It can lead to spasms and lack of coordination. The symptoms are usually caused by damage to or compression on the spinal cord. I remembered how I had slipped in Telly's birth stall and fell on him. Could it be my fault? Was it just that he was so big? Had he cracked his neck somehow in trailering? What had happened?

Still I waited to take him to Arizona Equine. My apprenticeship week was now underway, and with taking care of my own herd, arriving early at Linda's to work her horses, and do the long days of the workshops, I couldn't find a minute extra to trailer Telly anywhere. Not to mention deal with the news I might hear. I made an appointment for the end of the month, a few weeks out, and decided in the meanwhile I would talk with my colleagues at the workshop who were horse people also, and gather their feedback and ideas. Maybe someone had been through this before and had had a good outcome. Shelley the dreamer kept dreaming.

On the second day of the workshop, I took Linda aside to tell her that I thought I might have to put Telly down—end his life—if what was really wrong with him was something like Wobbler.

Linda listened and watched my face.

"Why don't you bring him here on Friday?" she said. "We can do a healing circle with him. Think about it. You and I can set it up." She stepped away to talk to another apprentice, leaving me to think.

I am not religious, but I am aware of the power of the spiritual world, and I honor it. I knew that a shamanic healing could be any of a broad range of practices performed by a shaman or practitioner, in order to help or heal another person. The methods, tools, symbols, and medicines might vary across cultures, but in general, the healing tried to make a three-way connection between the person, the shaman, and the universe, or spirit. In this case, Linda was offering me an opportunity for a healing of Telluride. I was willing to involve any higher power to help me with this horse I loved.

When Thursday came, I told Linda I wanted to bring Telly out. On Friday morning early, I loaded him into a trailer at my place, and made the fifty-minute journey with him. Linda and I put Telly in the round pen she used for the workshops to wait out the day. That evening we would ask the universe for assistance.

It is Thursday night before the healing, and I am dreaming that Telly is again a foal.

In the dream, I walk deep into a cave where he stands by himself, the white on his body glowing, the black masking parts of him into invisible night. I run my hands down his long thin legs to the teacup-sized hooves, over his small body, dark and light. I touch the whiskers on his nose with my fingertips. He is warm and smells of rain and wet earth.

I am sorry, little man, I say to him, *I came alone. I could not bring your future with me.*

He paws the cave floor and shakes his head from side to side, as if ridding himself of something he disagrees with. He steps past me. I feel insignificant to him. He passes through the cave entrance, and then turns to look back in at me. Once more, he scrapes the dirt with his hoof, as if drawing a line or some symbols that he dares me to cross over or be trapped behind forever. Raising his head and watching me, he starts to back up. He moves deeper into darkness and shadow, leaving me here alone.

I come to stand over the message he has left in dirt.

Blocky letters, as if written by a child.

What we lose defines us.

My apprenticeship group of fifteen people had been together by this time for three separate, solid weeks of that year, and we had become very close. We had created a space for each other in our lives that for want of a better word felt sacred, a protective place in which we could learn and be supportive of one another. As worried as I was for Telly, I felt comfort that this group of my friends and colleagues would stand together with me, at the very least to help me mourn the changes he was going through and that I was helpless to stop.

On Friday night, as the sun went down over the desert, we gathered in the main Epona house. Linda began the guided meditation for us. We closed our eyes, and with a blessing she opened our circle to the ancestor spirits, here the ancestor *horses*, and encouraged them to enter our space. The intention of our meditation—whether we asked a specific question of the air, or had a feeling come over us to which we wanted a response—was to encourage the ancestors to join and guide us. The responses we received would be as varied as the persons involved. It could be a feeling or a color or a smell. It could simply be a state of peace. Each individual needed to be very still and to focus if they were to recognize an answer in the thin air. Some of us might hear words in our minds, others might see images, and still others might feel nothing more than a breeze across a cheek and a sense of comfort and of being held in the space.

As a group, we all were asked to meditate on Telly, or more on his spirit energy, and call his spirit into the center of the room with us. Telly, the horse himself, stood just outside in his round pen under a quarter-moon sky.

I presented this question that would start Telly's shamanic journey.

Where do you want to go from here?

After twenty minutes of guiding our meditation, Linda paused and waited. She asked each of us to offer to the group what we felt or heard or saw during the experience of meditating on the spirit of Telly in the room. Of the fifteen apprentices, three graduated apprentices, Linda, and her staff's therapist—twenty people—every person but one said they had seen the color red in the images in their minds. The sole person who saw blue felt it might represent the hottest part of a fire, or the curative coolness of a spring. One of us said that the message coming to her was that this was a time of "change" for me and "healing" for Telly. Some of us got images of Telly talking to us, and telling us his own insight that his inability to do dressage was actually freeing him up to do this (Epona) kind of work. He said he wanted to do work to help *humans* become more whole. He said that he, himself, was fine. One of the apprentices, David, saw a red fire truck and an apple tree laden with crimson fruit. David then watched himself climb up into the apple tree, only to meet the water god Poseidon in the branches, who extended his arms and offered him an apple pie.

In the group, we also had one certified shamanic practitioner, named Eve. She spoke up last.

Eve said that in her images, she saw Telly being hit by lightning. She said that was why he had a neurological problem now. The electrical force of the strike had caused the damage.

When she stopped speaking, I lost my composure and burst into tears. Could it be? Lightning was always at play in the desert sky. Telly was so tall, standing in his paddock, and he stayed out all the time. Could it have happened and I didn't know it? Was it true? I didn't know what to believe. I also immediately felt that this ended my opportunity to believe he was okay—and I didn't want this confirmation that Telly might have a neurological problem. I just wanted him well. If I took in what Eve said even slightly, it might make it become real. I told myself this was only a meditation. Our minds make all kinds of pictures, that's all, pictures.

Linda saw me struggling and offered, "What would you ask Telly's spirit if you could?"

I thought two things: If he was hurt, I would ask for guidance on how to heal him. Or, to hold on to what was left of my previous Telly and how I wanted him to be, I would stand up and flee this circle of my friends and cry to the night until the morning took mercy on me and let me believe once more that Telly was well.

How could I stop weeping? How could I let him go? How could he go on hurting and still be the horse I knew? How. How. How.

When I could finally pull myself together enough to speak, I asked aloud to my young horse's spirit only one thing.

"How do you do this work?"

Only Telly could answer, and he would do that by showing me.

In the darkness, Linda led us out of the house and down the gravel to Telly's pen. The air was redolent with the perfumes of sage and desert dust. I opened the red pipe gate, went in to Telly, and slipped his halter onto his head. I attached a lead rope and stood quietly with him. What we would do next would come from Telly.

What I am going to tell you now is the truest thing I know.

The other members of the group stood outside the pen. Horses have no words, but I felt this animal tell me clearly that he wanted the group to come in and encircle him. So I used my own language to tell them to enter. They joined us, some coming in tentatively, and one by one formed a large circle of humans around him. One member reached for another's hands, then another, and soon the circle was completely joined, fingers intertwined, whether for comfort or because of the nature of the event upon us, I still don't know. As a horse person with years of experience, I *do* know that putting that many people around a giant four-year-old horse who kicks out unpredictably isn't a safe situation for the horse or the people. But they stood in that circle and Telly waited, quiet and calm. He had created that shape around him. He owned its energy.

The sky with its quarter moon was nearly starless, but what thin silver light the small moon gave was reflected off the tin roof of a nearby shed and gathered into a beam to shine focused onto a "vee" of white hair in the black hide on the left side of Telly's neck.

Some things we know in our souls are true regardless of what anyone might tell us. I knew without words that the lighted vee marked the very heart of the damaged nerve that was kissed by lightning.

It was dark and the white vee gleamed. We could feel the tension rising in us; too much coincidence can do that to a person. Again, without words, I felt Telly's energy draw everyone to him and specifically urge them to look at the lighted spot on his neck. He stood perfectly still while they tightened the circle around him.

Eve broke from her spot in the circle and came into the center with me and Telly. She asked if she could do a healing ritual with him. I stood without words to answer. Can I speak for a horse? Telly, as if in response to my thought, rotated his ears forward. It was as if he said *why not.*

Eve pressed close to his neck, where the vee-shaped light still marked the hide, and curled her hands together as if she held a tube. She blew breath through her hands onto the vee. She said a prayer over him, and he waited, calmly watching. When she finished and stepped back, I realized I had let the lead rope go slack so that it touched the ground. Telly started to move away from me, and I let him go, not thinking of safety or capture, just knowing his direction was chosen by him alone.

He first approached one person, and then the next, and then another. Here he touched one on the face with just the slightest press of his nose, breathed out, and then moved on. There he dropped his head over a shoulder, and touched that person on their back between their shoulder blades, and then moved on. Here he stopped at one of the men in our group, and literally licked his balding head, and then moved on. These actions were a kind of thanks given to each member for his or her participation in this circle.

Finally, he approached Anna, a member of our group who had undergone breast surgery three weeks before. He gently touched his nose to her chest, and then moved on to another person. I watched Anna's face, as did the others, and could see that only she didn't get the connection to Telly's location for his touch. After a few others in the circle, Telly returned to Anna, and this time he pushed his massive head into the spot where her surgery scar lay like a rude tattoo under her blouse. She burst into tears. On he went to Jessica, and touched her in the middle of her back. Did he know that this was where she had hurt herself when she fell off her horse, Dakota, weeks before—that she hadn't been on him since? Was Telly letting her know it was time to let go of this wound?

I know it to be so.

After Telly connected with every person, he was finished. Clearly his body posture changed back to one of a horse wanting to get on with the next thing. He stood by the gate of the pen, and as each person went out, she or he thanked him for the gifts he had given them. It could mean nothing else. We all knew.

By now it was pitch black. The moon no longer reflected off his hide. I loaded him onto the trailer, and he went in without event, as if nothing out of the ordinary had happened.

He wasn't really my horse any longer. He had been touched by a blessing so silent and wise I would have to allow him to be something else entirely.

Before this third week with my Epona group, I had made the appointment to take Telly to Arizona Equine, and I never kept it.

After the healing circle, I heard from Kathy, a member of my group. She sent me an e-mail asking if I'd gone to the appointment at the equine hospital, and how did it go? I wrote back that I didn't take Telly in, because I believed his new calling was to be a *medicine* horse. His job is to do this work he showed all of us that he is so good at, to call a circle of humans together and help them heal by standing with him, helping them let go of their fear, and accept the reality of things we can't see but that are. I told Kathy that I realized the only way he could take on this new work was if he had a physical issue that would give him permission to *not* become my competitive horse, and that would give me permission to see him in a new light. Otherwise, in my field, people would wonder why I had this beautiful horse that I didn't compete on. As a horse, his options were limited; he was bred to be a perfect dressage horse. His father, Eros, was a champion jumper. His mother, Laramie, was a Grand Prix dressage mare. Telluride had to manifest something, to *lose* something—one talent, one future—so that he wouldn't be pushed to become a competitive horse. I wrote that I believed that we all have ears to listen, and we tend to listen only to the words we speak. But we also need to listen with our eyes and our hearts, to be alert like a horse would be to the movement of great spirits in our midst.

My grandfather's abuse caused me to lose what might have been carefree in my childhood, my safety, and most of my ability to interact without worry with my own kind. And yet, because of this very loss, I have the life that led me to Telly, and am able to be here to tell this story to you. Some coincidences are too canny to be random.

What Telly lost defines him now. He will be my therapy horse as I move forward in my work with humans and healing. He is gentle, kind, and though enormous, will easily bring his head to your level to listen closely to your breath. He is a medicine horse of great power. I am honored to be his partner.

My horses are always very clear about their position in a herd, and offer this advice to me in my own human circle: *Wait and be mindful of those stronger and weaker than you are.*

They give me guidance for integrating someone new into my life. *Give the new member a suitable amount of time to watch and evaluate you before you interact with them out of instinct or fear.*

My horses are very clear with their boundaries. *If you approach me and I have never been touched by a human I trust, and you think you will succeed in touching me, the joke's on you. I'll laugh halfway across the paddock before you can extend your hand.*

The process of building trust in a person or an animal is very long and trying on both creatures. I have always felt that if I only had one horse to work and it was a wild mustang that this process would be quicker than with any other horse. Why? Because I could spend all my time building trust from the ground up. But in truth, no horse or person is quick to offer you their trust. Healing is a process of knowing that it takes a very long time to trust, to do this work, and to be comfortable with ourselves. It will take as long as we need it to take. But it can happen.

I trust Telly not to throw me if he can help it, and to accept the work I'll put him through to keep him sound. He trusts I'll be there for him, and will let him become the horse he must be. It isn't mine to pick his work. He's done that. I trust he is right. And when the time comes that the lightning in his hide calls him back to the night sky, I'll be there to hold him, head on my lap, as he closes his eyes and sighs his last. That is my job. I am his voice.

In the art of dressage riding, the serpentine is the simplest of ways to move across an arena. The horse and rider divide the arena into thirds, and traverse it in a sine wave, gently undulating and changing direction back onto the curve itself. No different from the snake as she retraces her path, and then advances toward her future. The curve gives horse and rider the chance to balance, and the opportunity to rebalance, again and again as they wind. The future that the serpentine leads horse and rider to is a single perfect stride attained in a string of other footfalls. In this one stride horse and human move together, less separate than before.

I trace the serpentine of my life with my horses, and am grateful to come back to them.

Echo, the round little mare who tolerated my early "kick and pull days" of riding without skill, showed me that the way out of my childhood nightmares was on the back of a horse. She was willing to run with me as long and as far as I needed to go. I still ride her in my thoughts when I am scared or fleeing disaster in my day.

Innovation and Reflection, my first competitive horses, gave me a reason to leave Michigan, to go west, and to become a professional. They were the pillars of my professional horse life. Two athletes, two good friends.

Billie Joe Freckles, the first Grand Prix Appaloosa in the United States, gave me his speckled back on which to sharpen my talent, and a sweet taste of success. He nurtured me emotionally and provided for me financially. He gave me my time with Chuck Grant, whom I still miss. I sold Billie Joe and lost myself to the aftermath of losing part of a dream, but losing him defined me, too.

Kingston offered me the chance to see that the horse I think I need to move my career ahead, and the one that needs me, are different animals, but who can both take me where I want to go. It is always about choices. The road is just a little different when you accept the horse that needs you.

Renaissance, once my own wily pinto mare, gave me her focus when I did a thing right. When we listen, we can understand the speaker—no matter the language or species. Listening is hard. Renaissance, as my horse, and then belonging to another, worked to teach me and all of her riders the art of paying close attention to what matters.

Cosmic, though mine only as he transited from Dora and then to Sara, loved unconditionally anyone who showed him kindness. That is curative for a weary heart. It's not easy to forgive and return love to the ones that hurt me, intentionally or not. But out in the Northwest there is a big gray horse who would tell me life goes on and you have to keep trying. Somewhere green grass awaits you.

Avatar, a latecomer in my barn, came free to me from a previous owner. Still in my herd, he has reaffirmed for me that you can never tell what a horse, or a person, can do unless you risk asking. I risk it now in my work with those persons willing to take a chance to let a horse help them experience a dream that tastes true, sometimes bitter, and always rich.

Laramie shows me daily that I have to work hard to make my perfect horse become real, and that hope often puts us on a path that leads where we least expect it. I still ride her daily but with a sense now that if we don't achieve the higher levels of our work, we still have the rides to cherish between us, and time is treasure.

Eros, with Laramie, brought me Telly, tall man with a tricky fin.

And Telluride?

He is my shaman, my friend, and my blessing. I heal in his presence.

Epilogue

Every horse trainer has a method. Every program that examines how we can communicate with and ride horses more naturally, or that attempts to incorporate them as therapy animals, varies in purpose and approach. Every horse brings to us an intuitive intelligence that can teach us something valuable about building community among ourselves.

Linda Kohanov and her instructors and staff at the Epona Center, where I now work, are engaged in this examination of learning about the intuitive intelligence of the Epona herd, not only to assist the clients who come to the workshops here, but as a place where professional horse people can learn from this innate horse intelligence something key to creating an authentic community of human *and* horse.

In the summer of 2005, I closed my Dressage Center, where I had been training competitive dressage clients and their horses for eighteen years, to work full-time with Linda at the Epona Center in Sonoita, Arizona. Linda had just relocated Epona to its new home, moving her herd and staff from just outside of Tucson to this 130-acre ranch. When she asked me to manage the ranch, and have the opportunity to continue my work as an Epona instructor on site and offer dressage training to those who attend the programs here, I accepted. I could taste the depth of my own tiredness of dressage competition, and desire to immerse myself in the well-being of horses and the connections they can afford for healing with humans.

I knew I wouldn't be the only trainer, or the only Epona instructor, and it was a big ranch to run. I had no idea how much I would be asked to change and stretch. I would have to join a human herd—a community of trainers, therapists, and clients, with whom I would learn to integrate my techniques, observe others, and learn more daily from the horses themselves. After thirty years of horse work, mostly running my own business, I had thought there might be nothing truly new in, or under, any saddle. But the work I get to do now, with these horses and people, breaks unique ground.

The Epona Center at Apache Springs Ranch lies in a green and gold canyon, blessed with good springs of water, informative ravens, docile cattle, and the Epona herd. The ranch itself has a Western history that I am just coming to know. Its human ghosts likely "broke" their horses in the old ways, rather than gentling them using today's methods. I don't fault those men and women—it was a different time. Recently, I struck up a conversation with a town local who told me he knew the ranch history well, and that there is a "bone dump" on the place that holds the remains of horses and other livestock used and gone. I haven't found it yet, but I do wonder what stories the bones of those horse ghosts might share, and what they think of the new work here.

The spirit of the Epona work can be summarized as a realization that we need to change the paradigm of how humans and horses interact. The ranch offers us a living laboratory to test what works and doesn't. As humans with a past in the horse industry, we bring along old patterns and negative practices that we have assimilated into ourselves and our training, but here we must confront this experience and see if it is sustainable in a community that aims for truthful, authentic interactions. We can't continue to teach here the way we did before. It won't work because we can't be islands of expertise—we must share and exchange truthfully. And hardest of all—we have to get along with each other.

That's not easy when accomplished trainers with strong egos and their own styles come to work together. We struggle to accept each other's approaches and often go through an intense negotiation process just to co-exist. For example, something as simple as using the crossties in the barn while preparing for daily work creates conflict—who gets to use them first? Why? I might expect a generous *no, really, Shelley, you go first* attitude among these humans who have endured a lot and chosen to come here and work together, or to be very generous myself automatically because of the common goal of authentic community. But it doesn't happen that way easily. It can't be about *I'm the real trainer, get out of my way.* Even if that feels more natural to each and every one of us.

Sometimes, no matter the effort we take, we can't compromise. In those cases, we work hard to find a way for each person to feel empowered and have the space she needs in which to train *her* way. For example, when we moved to the ranch, we had an outdoor arena, an indoor arena, and one round pen—and 130 acres of open space. But a round pen and the small space it encircles is where the action is—it's the trainer's essential space. I like to keep my round pen dynamic. In it, I keep a beach ball and horse toys and a cavaletti (a pole that has x–shaped end pieces on which you can turn the pole so that it can be at different heights off the ground) to incorporate play and the opportunity to jump the cavaletti into the horses' work with me. Another Epona trainer wants a more meditative emptiness in her round pen space. We tried to share, she tossing my toys out, and me putting them back onto the dirt, but sometimes, the best way to accommodate two trainers is to have separate spaces, or two round pens. As horses in a herd separate naturally, but respect the space each might occupy (as long as you respect that I *have* a place in the herd), we co-exist and can work.

We try hard not to say to one another *I don't believe in that way of training* or *that device or that technique never works* because, frankly, it could be true that it works in some instances, despite our opinion or experience or prejudice. However, as Linda has said, "Just because it works for a particular trainer doesn't mean I have to run over and adopt it."

So why all this negotiation? Because what we do here has to be in the best interest of the horse, and finally, in a reversal of roles, it is up to the humans to adapt. By changing how we communicate with each other more truthfully, and acknowledging our human defenses, we are prepared to learn to communicate with the horses from truth. They can tell instantly what emotion you bring to the day, if your training request has a subtext of anger or frustration, or if you are just not interested in the work with them. To be effective for the others who come to Epona in their search for authenticity, everyone here has to be open to the horses as colleagues. The first lesson they offer is that survival depends on your herd, and your interactions with its members.

A belief in the intuitive intelligence of our horses informs the work at Epona. It's not easy to admit that a horse might be not only a gentle, nurturing animal from whom we can draw comfort and examples of strength and straightforward behavior. They might actually have access to information we can't see or touch—instinctual and intelligent intuition. Their intuition works on many levels, and I don't fully understand all of them (I cannot *be* horse). But I know from watching that if we pay attention to the clues they give us about how their intuition works, we might encounter a new way be with them, and then can take that information back into our human relationships to achieve something very good.

To show you how this intuition operates, I need to return to the imagery seen by everyone who participated in Telly's guided meditation, which occurred more than nine months before Epona's relocation.

At the time, Linda and her husband Steve Roach were seeking a new piece of property to move Epona to. They found Apache Springs Ranch, then an Arabian horse ranch, in Gardner Canyon in the early spring of 2005. It is drier than ever before in Arizona, and not every plant thrives in this sere and thirsty environment. Unusual for Arizona, someone had long ago planted apple trees here. Apple trees need water and a good frost to produce fruit. You might get the frost, but the water is all about hope in this landscape. The ranch owner at the time told Linda that not only did the trees bear excellent apples, but a nearby neighbor was used to collecting the fruit and making apple pies for everyone. If Linda and Steve were lucky, she said, the same might happen for them.

Shortly after Linda and Steve put an offer on the property, the entire mountain behind it caught fire. For long terrifying days, fire trucks roared up and down the dirt road above the ranch pumping out precious water trying to extinguish disaster. The apple trees and the ranch survived.

Weeks later on a perfect indigo evening, after another long day of moving human and horse gear in, Linda and I sat out in garden chairs, sipping a well-earned, move-in-blues cocktail. We'd been silent for a little bit, tired and dirty from chores. Then Linda leaned forward in her chair.

"Do you recall the images from Telly's journey?" she asked.

And I was instantly there in that night circle of my memory.

"The fire truck, and the color red," I responded. "All but one of us saw red, and the only other color was blue."

"The apple tree. Red apples, red fire trucks. Poseidon, god of water, blue. Apple pie." she said.

You know that tingly feeling on the back of your neck when you realize something true.

Was it simple coincidence? I wasn't sure, though the alignment of exact images and events was uncanny. Did Telly, with an intuitive intelligence I might dismiss because he does not speak *my* language, see past and future?

Linda and I have talked a long time about how so very much about coming to this property is like that. After an experience like the fire and Telly's premonition, she asks, how can I not listen to my horses? I struggle with it, but the coincidences keep occurring, and she and I have learned to pay attention to the horses for their insights, and regularly discuss them, especially the outcomes.

For example, Telly recently came up lame with a quarter crack, which is a crack on the inside of his front hoof, and which ended the small riding work I had just put him back to. These cracks are hard to heal. Now, letting horses go barefoot, or pulling off their shoes, is a late-blooming passion in the horse world. In nature, horses *are* barefoot; in human practice and use, we shoe them. When Telly was at Lee's barn for training, and I let her persuade me that I should pull his shoes, he immediately went lame. My farrier lit into me that

I should know better with a horse of his size. But now with a quarter crack, I wondered, what good would the shoes really do?

I knew Telly would be lame for a long while as the hoof grew down and healed. This was an opportunity for an intuition test— maybe Telly had an opinion about his shoes. One morning, feeding, I hopped off the Gator cart at the end of a lane next to the pasture Telly was in. He grazed several acres away at the front of the pasture with his herd mates. I leaned over the fence and sent him a thought, *Come to the back of this pasture if you want those shoes off.*

Within a minute or two, he raised his head, turned, and ambled toward me in that easy swinging way that only a big horse can, one long leg hitting ground after another. He stopped at the fenceline near me. Lucky coincidence maybe. So I sent another thought. *If you really want me to take off your shoes, hang your head over the fence and lick and chew.* He walked closer to the fence, put his head over, and did. That afternoon I called the farrier and we pulled the shoes.

But a quarter crack is nothing to play with, coincidence or not. I still worried, based on his last barefoot experience, that I'd have him lame and suffering in nothing flat. I ordered a pair of Boa boots, plastic boots that protect the entire hoof. Within a day, he'd broken one and lost it somewhere in the huge pasture. I immediately thought I would try to replace it. But as clearly as if he had held a picture in front of me, I visualized him with both boots off. Could it be that he wanted me to take the other boot off as well?

I returned to his pasture and undid the remaining boot. He's remained sound ever since. As I stood there holding the boot, watching him walk away from me back to his pals, barefoot, he stopped and looked back, then continued. His look seemed to say, *You're starting to get the picture.*

How many coincidences do we need, to consider that some of these might not be coincidences at all? Linda is quick to explain that we don't act on every whimsical notion we get around the Epona horses. But we really do test what we hear or feel so that we can get a sense of whether they might be communicating for real, and how they do it.

For most of my first year here, I've worked my mare Laramie in the usual dressage ways: suit her up with saddle, bridle, and boots, grab my helmet and dressage whip, and head for the arena. We school for about forty-five minutes, and then after taking her tack off, I return her to her pasture. She can, and does, literally pull me along by her lead rope down the road to her pasture unless I use a chain around her nose to provide a little added "ahem" pressure. I had an insight one day that maybe she would benefit from one of the Epona exercises. What if, after a traditional workout, I brought her to my round pen and asked her to "join up" with me (approach me as a herd member), as I expect any Epona therapy horse to do?

Laramie is a big mare, and highly competitive. She's no cinch to handle on the ground. At first, she thought the round pen was terrific fun, but she wasn't exactly joining up. I asked her to travel around the pen, which included several times over the cavaletti. Finally, tired and happy, she dropped her head a bit, licked and chewed, and slowing to a walk, came into my space. Her response is not magic. Many of us do this with our horses. But I think Laramie considers *this* as a stress reliever after her dressage work, so that she can decompress and let off the energy she's accumulated from concentrating on the high-level dressage movements. After incorporating this into her routine work for five consecutive days, I found her easy to walk back to her pasture on a long lead line without the chain. On the sixth day, I took her straight from dressage arena to pasture, no round pen work. She was a machine, pulling me along, all over again. The lesson for me was clear as daylight.

What's different now in Laramie and in me? Before I thought that if I took my competitive horse out of her usual work, it would take her attention off and affect the quality of her dressage movements. In reality she can do this connecting work as well, and *still* be ready to compete. In fact, maybe this connecting work is the important link. And not just for Laramie.

I know that my own routine as a dressage competitor was to hole up on my property and work and work over the tests to be sure I was ready for a show. I didn't take a break to relax and find my human center, or try to connect with other humans to soothe the stress. When I came to Epona, I lost my routine—drilling in dressage work for competition—and my highly competitive nature had to face the new work of connecting with the other humans in Epona instead. Laramie has shown me that there is a restorative quality to doing something completely different. I am different because of my work at Epona. If I compete again, and I suspect I will, I've got a new outlook on how to prepare. Laramie and I, in intuitive synchronicity, have proven it.

Linda's intuition is also benefiting the stallions at the ranch. We have begun a stallion handling and socialization program that aims to bridge the exile stallions experience in traditional breeding operations, and the fear in handling them that arises when we experience their powerful individuality and remoteness from us. We have routinely kept them separated out of a herd and from their own kind to make it easier to handle them and to limit breeding to our schedule only. Having worked with stallions much of my life and now handling Linda's stallions Merlin and Spirit, I concur with Linda that there is a better way to connect with these intense horse energies.

We are trying a program to bring a stallion and his owner into each other's presence in a way that is safe and respectful of both horse and human. It entails learning how to approach the energy of a stallion, who is very sensitive and aware of shifts in emotion. It includes understanding the work the stallion will do—like all of us, they need to do something, not just stand around in an isolated pen. In addition, Linda has tested giving Merlin a herd, placing Rasa and Comet with him and allowing him to interact and breed with them at will. Of course, not every one of us can or should do this, but Epona is a laboratory. We know we are only recreating what is natural in the wild. But here, *we* are learning to be a part of the stallion's herd as well.

Horses—regardless of whether they are stallions or Grand Prix dressage mounts or even just older souls who can only do reflective ground work with clients—will all join in this work with humans because we treat them and respect them as colleagues. The horse has a role to influence the human through its insight into our emotion and energy, as we influence them with our training and consistency. We're finding the horses take more of an interest in their life with us because they have renewed interest in their jobs. We are partners.

The biggest challenge for an authentic community of horses and trainers and clients and therapists is finding a way to run a commercial horse operation that is not just humane for its people and horses, but that is actually nourishing for everyone. It's something the horse world doesn't see very often.

As horse people, we know the abuse the traditional system of training can inflict on us. As we come up as apprentice trainers, we may be screamed at, or treated like we are in a military boot camp. If your opinion differs on how best to work with a horse, either you or your horse might be punished for it. It's amazing for us to see how hard that is to overcome in our own work here. We default to old patterns. We really have to work hard to treat each other humanely. We of course treat the paying clients well. But we also have to be clear and set boundaries with them, so that we don't take out our frustrations or exhaustion on each other after spending emotion-filled therapy days with them. We have even had to caution our male workers not to try and hit on the female employees. It might be human nature, but here it is a very big deal, especially in the safe and nurturing environment we're trying to foster for the clients and each other.

Some clients come to Epona to heal whatever horrible horse trauma or life trauma they have had. Others come to study training and handling horses in a different way. And still others, horse people, come here trying to get over a horse-world trauma that has a human as the cause. If you can get a truly accomplished horse person to be secure in their being and their art form, they don't need to run down their students or horses. They can take that back out in the horse world and make a difference. The late and respected dressage trainer, Reiner Klimke, insisted at a clinic I attended that the footing be dragged in the arena more than once a day so that all horses and riders got an equal chance to ride on the best surface and succeed. Why don't we think like that more often, I wonder.

As we work with professional and amateur horse people here, we are encouraged to try and always be conscious of those moments when anyone feels threatened in our work, and try to convey, "Hey, I'm secure in who I am and I can enjoy taking a student to a new level, rather than keeping you below me." We all agree to work on calling our peers aside to relate what we observe, good and bad. We also make an agreement with each other to follow up and have compassion for each other when we act out, and make mistakes, or have a stressful moment and fall back to old behavior.

And so bad patterns of behavior happen less frequently among the staff now than a year ago, and each of us can catch our behavior more quickly and change it. But the reality is that Linda has brought people to Epona who are unique and innovative—they're not all speaking the same training language, and as hard as that is to negotiate, human to human, it also has real value. Our challenge is to appreciate the time it takes one trainer to understand the benefits of another trainer's method. It's hard enough that we each speak a different training language to the horses—learning to speak to each other in common, humane *human* does not happen overnight. Enter the horses at Epona.

Amazingly, despite the fact that we have words to communicate with and horses don't, the horses understand the humans and our interactions better and faster than we ever do. We had a Canadian thoroughbred, Cali, in for training at the old Epona location who hadn't been ridden since we moved in to the new ranch. Susan Mayfield, another trainer here, was doing the ground and body work getting the horse ready for riding, and I would do the training in the saddle. One day, a volunteer staff member came to fill in for Susan and do her ground work. I asked that she not put Cali away right after she finished, because I would need to ride him, and then he would be ready and warmed. Because the ground work was done, my riding work went so much easier. However, the humans involved, Susan and the volunteer, weren't happy that I was going to ride him on the same day as his ground work, because their mode was to separate ground work days from riding days. But horses adapt in a second to what's going to happen next, which is why the riding work was easy. We are so much slower to accept a change. Still, conveying that ease of work to Susan did give her insight into the horse, and I emphasized the benefit of her ground and body work with Cali on his under-saddle work.

As humans, we can be blind to most of what's going on around us, and extremely rigid and judgmental with each other. Not with the horses, where we've hung the halos, but with our human partners. If we could find a way to become more horse-like with other humans, we would be more adaptable—to adjust to what is happening and understand what is under the words people speak. We're starting to do it here at the new Epona ranch, but it has taken months and people who are courageous enough to do the work here and be vulnerable and admit that there is still much to learn.

Negotiating an authentic community of horses and humans is an evolving process. Linda and I wish there were more horse trainers willing to open their toolboxes and add in more insight in this way, to work in a community of trainers, as we do here. You can only remain separate and assume you have some higher value if you stay in your own barn. If you're going to work in a training cooperative like Epona, you have to be okay with what's going on under your own skin. You have to be open to the sureness that you don't know everything, and simultaneously be secure enough in what you *do* know to share it or practice it with regard for your peers. You also need to learn to respect that your intuition is right when it lets you know you need to ask for help. In a community, you will become a member of a herd. A herd relies on its individuals, separately and collectively, to find sustenance. In an authentic human herd, we need to rely on each other for knowledge, tolerance, and the grace to share our experiences. In a drought, any one of us might be just the one to remember where to paw the earth to reveal a spring. From that spring, together, we might drink in something true.

CPSIA information can be obtained at www.ICGtesting.com
Printed in the USA
LVOW081725040113

314415LV00004B/609/A